GIVING BIRTH TO YOUR

HOME-BASED

BUSINESS

GROW YOUR BUSINESS AND STILL HAVE TIME
FOR YOURSELF, FAMILY, AND FRIENDS

By: Debbie Porter

Published: 2017

ISBN 13: 978-1548021030

ISBN 10: 1548021032

LCCN: TK

DISCLAIMER

Cover Design: Faiqdesigner

Editing: Kim Porter

FOREWORD

I am a retired NFL Super Bowl, All-Pro-running back for the New York Giants and I spent most of my career working with great teammates to make touchdowns and wins for my team. I am fortunate to have led my team to a Super Bowl championship. None of this would have happened without the training I received from my many coaches over the years.

Now, I have an opportunity to introduce you to one of my off the field coaches, Debbie Porter, who also happens to be my sister. Debbie, or Deb as I call her, was instrumental in helping negotiate my contract with the New York Giants and for directing me through the maze of decisions that I had no clue how to make.

She has always been wise. When we were younger, she possessed an uncanny ability to be a great role model for me and my siblings. Deb's excellent business and life knowledge, helped me to navigate the NFL and several businesses, and remain a grounded sibling, son, father and husband.

Rodney Hampton

TABLE OF CONTENTS

WHY I WROTE THIS BOOK "THE NUDGE"

Do You Remember How It All Started?

It's almost a mirage, here I am, after a couple of decades, having survived all the stages of motherhood, along with owning my own home-based business. You would think now that both of my children are off to college, I would just chill and do nothing. Believe me, I tried.

I'm sure you know all too well when you are supposed to be doing something else with your time; with your life. You know the feeling when it is time to move on to another level, but you ignore it like you don't feel that nudge. Well that was exactly what I tried to do, to ignore the nudge. I have been asking myself why on earth am I writing this book. Why won't this nudge leave me alone?

The nudge kept saying, *"It's needed."*

I kept asking "What's needed?"

"Your book," the nudge replied.

Who needs it I asked? (Oh yes, I'm talking to the nudge).

The nudge said, *"She does."*

I asked, again "Who?"

The nudge said "*Her.*" Do you know who the nudge said needed this book? It was "YOU." Yes, you.

You are the reason, I haven't been able to sleep, and you are that reason I can't just sit still and watch a TV show without uncovering a problem, creating a solution, a book topic or title. You are the reason. "**Me?**" *Yes, you*, **Y- O- U!** You are the person I am writing this book for. It is you that have kept me up for many nights, some of which I have spent intensely asking for help. It is you, for whom I have made all these mistakes, so you wouldn't have to make them again. It is you, for whom I pray that God would let know, that all things are possible. It is you that I had to go through all of this for. It is you, that I have to remind that your great dreams can be achieved. It is you that I need to let know that you can have a business, a home-based business at that. And that you can survive it, and still have time for yourself, family and friends. Yes, it is you.

Entrepreneurs are gifts to this world. Clay Clark, CEO of Thrive 15 says "An entrepreneur is someone who seeks to profitably solve a problem that the world has, in exchange for monetary compensation to achieve their dreams." The entrepreneurial spirit is a gift that inspires others to become the best they can be. Does any of this sound like you, or does any of this describe you in any form or fashion? That's because YOU ARE THE DEFINITION OF AN EN-TREPRENEUR. Fortunately, I am an entrepreneur also, and I want to inspire you to become the best entrepreneur that you can be.

You are in familiar territory if someone, be it a friend, family member or a co-worker, has told you that you should start your own business. Those who possess an innate entrepreneurial ability are often recognized by others for our potential and told to start our own businesses; essentially implying, that we don't belong where we are anymore. This is the stark truth. They aren't even telling you something that you don't already know. I know, I hear you. I hear you asking the same questions which I have asked repeatedly. *How in the world will I do it all? How can I pull this off?* This job currently helps to pay the bills; however, my real job, my actual job, starts the moment I get home. This scenario is a snap shot of your life:

You stop by the store to figure out what you can cook quickly. You pick up the children from school, and stay home just long enough to have them change their clothes. You take them both to gymnastic practice. "God please let me make it there in time so they can get rid of some of this energy! "You flip-flop between the gymnastic classes of both the five-year-old and the three-year-old. After an hour, you finally get home to your back-breaking routine of cooking, and taking them outside to play for an hour or so while the food is cooking. Next, you bring them inside to feed them, bathe them, and lay out their clothes for the next day while they are in the bathtub FOREVER. Oh, Thank God for bath time! You get them out, and dress them for bed. You pray with them, read with them, and kiss them goodnight. Of course, you've got to go downstairs to clean the kitchen, and clean up all the toys. Get everything ready for tomorrow. Go take a bath. Get in the bed and prepare to do it all again tomorrow. Oh, my God! You almost scream out. Your exhaustion level is extremely intense!

Well, the truth is, I just described my life. The exact way it would play out daily when my children were younger. *What did you say?* This sounds a lot like your day, except that you have boys and instead of gymnastics; you had to go for football practice? Hmmm, I did not hear you. What did you ask? Am I married? Yes, I am, and before you ask, I'd like to tell you that he is a wonderful man, a police officer; an undercover officer at that, as if I need some more stress in my life! During that stage in my life, he worked from

11-7p.m., 12-8p.m., 2-10p.m. or some crazy weird shift that I can't even remember. Although we had been married for almost 10 years at that time, I felt like a single parent. I usually could not wait to go to work, which ironically, was where I would go to get some rest! Work? Please, that was a piece of cake. I really didn't even have to think there. I was just going through the motions.

If you haven't figured it out by now, I have had other businesses; but this home-based business is what has absolutely made my life easier at this stage of my life. You're about to give birth to your business. You are about to discover how all of my mistakes can help you. You are finally about to be given some help as to how to make all of this happen. Remember, you are the reason I had to write this book and I know you are interested. I know that I am talking to you because with all that you have to do, you should have stopped reading by now. Let me correct that: you would have never picked up this book if there wasn't something yearning in you to get the business started. Now, let's get to it!

FIRST
TRIMESTER

CHAPTER 1
THE CONCEPTION PLAN

Flowing in line with this book's title, I'd like us to consider the *birthing process*. Everyone knows how this works, both men and women. I'd like to point out that yes, men and women understand it from differing angles, but men still understand! The first step is that intense desire to birth a child and from now onwards, we're going to call your business a Baby. Your Baby.

In planning to conceive, we may not get to choose whether we get a girl, boy, both or triplets. Nor can we design what they look like or which talents they're born with. With a business, however, we have a lot more control on the front end. Planning may be what kind of business, when we want it to mature, whether we have saved money to support this new business through the startup times, who else we need in our lives to help us run our lives (and/or jobs) and tend to our new Baby. Planning is making room in our lives for the Baby business. And yes, we will go on to *conceive it, carry it* and *deliver it*. However, let's not move too fast, it's all a process!

First things first. What does it take to have a baby? Yes, you got it right SEX. And you must have it when the ladies are ovulating, to ensure there will be conception. The next almost logical question, is do we just want to have sex, or do we want to make love? What, too much? Get over yourself and go with me. Let us assume your husband has worked all day long, let's pick the 3p.m. -11p.m. shift. You saw the schedule earlier with the children, you said it was like your schedule, so let's go with that. You picked them up from school and took them to activities. You have done the cooking, cleaning, bathing and preparation for tomorrow. You have taken your bath and finally laid your tired body down, in your cold bed. Imagine, you are in a deep sleep when your husband gets home. You feel him kiss you on your cheek, and go to the shower. When he comes to bed and scoots under you, you want to say *Noooo*!!! What, not you, you want me to? Honey, you have no idea how tired I am. You can go through the list again of all that you have done today. And that is after a full day's work. You can truly justify why you're tired and why you don't want to have sex.

Or you could take an alternative route. You could decide to remember all the wonderful reasons for which you love him, all the things that you love about him. You can appreciate that he goes to work every day. You can remember that he takes the kids out on Saturdays so you can finally have some me time. You can remember that he gets up to cook breakfast every Saturday morning, wash the dishes, and wash clothes. You can remember that no matter how tired he is, he gets up and goes to church on Sundays with his family, and usually off to a birthday party or family function afterward. In summary, all the reasons why you would want to have sex with him. Now that changes things.

Now, as he gets into bed and gently kisses you on your back, on your cheek, your neck; you smile because you can smell his cologne. You now want to have his baby or at least, you want to have fun trying. *Oh, Mom, Dad, Dana and Devin;* skip this part I know you don't want to hear this. Lol. As my children would say, TMI.

Back to what I was saying. You don't want to just have sex, you want to make love and we both know, that these are two different things. You don't want this to be a duty. You want to hunger for him as much as he does for you. You don't want to rush it, because you're tired, or you're sleepy. You want it to last. If you are going to have to take a shower in the morning, it might as well be worth it! If you're going to have a busy day, you might as well have a smile on your face. As my grandmother would say "Lord a Mercy!" Sorry, I lost focus for a moment. I'm back.

Back to the business. That is what you must do to get your business up and running, to get your Baby off the ground. You can't just want a business, you have got to love, love, love, what you are about to do. Starting this business should be like making love to the man you love. You should anticipate working on your business. You should carve out time for your business, and you should never be too busy for your business. You should look at your Baby across the room and smile. You should think about your Baby and just smile. Just the thought of your Baby makes you happy.

You know, I don't ever remember my dad not having a business. I do remember him having a *job* and a *business*. He would work from 6am until 2p.m. He would get off work just to go back to work; this time it was to work on his business. He has had all types of businesses, and there was one common thread; HIM. He consistently exhibited an amazing work ethic along with his ability to love and believe in whatever business he was doing at the time. I believe to this day, that he can sell a snow cone to an Eskimo. He had five children, five active children, and I never ever remember him complaining about having to work. What I do remember is that he invested more time in his business than he did his job. He knew something that I did not know at the time. He knew that he did not want to depend on someone else for his livelihood. So, as Les Brown would say, he did what other people wouldn't do, to have what other people wouldn't have.

As I mentioned earlier, my dad would leave his job at 2p.m., just to go to work on his Baby. One of his businesses was a vending machine business and a game room known as **Hampton Amusement**. He had vending machines all around town, along with pool tables, jukeboxes, air hockey games, etc. If you had a bar, club, game room, diner or any other type of business that required a vending machine, **Hampton Amusement** had you covered! And oh my God, after Pac-Man and Donkey Kong arcade game became popular we were making the big bucks. I know, I'm telling my dad's age right. More than that, I am telling my age. LOL!

I remember him getting off work, going around to all locations to either collect his money, or to repair the machines. Then he would probably have some event he had to attend. Possibly, one of my brothers' basketball games, especially since I had three brothers who happened to be on three different teams! One was on the freshmen team, one on Jr. Varsity and one on the Varsity. Yes, that came out to a minimum of six games a week. I don't like watching basketball today for this reason. My dad and mom were always in the stands. He always drove his own truck because he usually had to go back to work after the game.

When he would finally get home, he would go to bed around 10p.m., I often remember, his pager going off at midnight or one in the morning, because one of the jukeboxes may have stopped working and he had to go repair it. There I go telling my age again-- *I was a toddler I don't know how I remember any of this.* Lol. Anyway, he would get up and go fix the jukebox. Can't have a party without music, now can you? More importantly, we didn't want them to, because we got paid for every song that played. I just realized we were the DJ. Anyway, my dad would get out of the bed to go fix the machines, come back, and go to bed just to get up, to be at work for 6 a.m. Did he complain? No. He did what he had to do to keep his Baby happy. He carved out time for his Baby because he knew the long hours and sacrifices were only temporary.

Well, a couple of years later, the company my dad worked for started laying off people. Finally, the day came and my dad got laid off. We thought he would have been upset, but he was excited. "*Wheee*!" he said, "No more job, I'm FREE!" My dad had worked there for more than 20 years, yet he was too young to retire. What we did not know is that he was praying to get laid off. He was able to keep his insurance, get a severance package, and still get paid for a while; which allowed him time to grow his business and replace his full-time income.

When he got laid off, he was excited that he could finally give his Baby the attention it deserved. He would get up and work on his Baby as if it were a full-time job. Because you know what, it was. It had become both his full time, and part time job. I would type up the song names and label them in the machine, put records in order, keep all his record books, so we would know what machines he had in which locations. We would wrap up all the money, all coins. Until this day, I can look at a stack of quarter, dimes, or nickels and know if one is missing out of the roll. That's how often we counted and rolled coins. That's also how my siblings and I made some of our extra money; we knew that for every roll that did not have enough to fill, we would get a chance to split it. We would pray for the quarters and dimes because there was $10 in every quarter roll and $5 in each dime roll. We knew that on top of giving us the incomplete rolls, he would also give each of us a roll of nickels and that was $2 each. That was the beginning of our ***first home-based business***. Go figure!!!

I said all of that to say, I have not known life without a business being in it. We have always had a home-based business and I just did not realize that's what it was. I have lived and breathed this stuff all my life and I absolutely love it. I love identifying problems, and finding solutions to them. Knowing all this, I hope you can allow yourself to let me guide you through the steps to conceive, carry, and deliver your Baby. Let me help you find the tools and energy to have time for it all: God, your husband, your children, your extended family, your friends, and your Baby.

Regardless of what type of home-based business you choose, you must start by taking the time to conceive it. Yes, it can be done, I did not say that it would be easy, and I did not say that it would be cheap. I did not say that you would not be tired. I am simply telling you that it can be done. I am telling you that I can help you attain success with less stress.

This book is filled with insight on how to make sure your Baby is ready for the real world. By reading this book in its entirety, you will become aware of the various stages of your Baby's growth. It's just like when you are pregnant and you go through all the different stages and varying emotions. By reading this book, you will become better prepared for what to expect. You will be better prepared when you open the doors for business. The difference is that you have a built-in nanny, me of course, and you haven't even given birth.

Meanwhile, I would have you concentrate on simply having intense sex/making love so you can conceive your Baby. I will work to help you remove any obstacle that might get in the way of you conceiving. I will make sure that you keep your stress level low. Stress is not your friend and it can prevent you from getting pregnant. I am not going to start the business for you, however, I am going to guide you in the right direction so you won't be so stressed out. While you are trying to conceive, I am going to be your four-leaf clover. Let's not stress out over all the things that you need for a business, we are going to work together to get through all those steps!

Who exactly am I? As I said earlier, think of me as that nanny you have before the baby even gets here. You just relax, and enjoy mating time. Let's just take it one day at a time.

TAKEAWAYS for The Conception Plan:

- Be sure you choose a business that you can be passionate about
- Understand the sacrifices that will be necessary to give birth to your Baby (your business)
- As soon as you can, dedicate your full-time work efforts and attention to your business
- Allow me to be your built-in nanny and help you through this birthing process so that you can have success with less stress

CHAPTER 2

CONGRATULATIONS: YOU'RE HAVING A BABY!

Congratulations!!!! I see you did the work, and I hope you had fun doing it. So, you have conceived your Baby. You are now pregnant. You know that you are having a Baby, and now the work begins.

This is the stage where you know you are pregnant; maybe about four weeks in but you don't feel pregnant. There are no real signs. This is the foundation, and we have got to make it through these next three months. Others may not even know you are pregnant yet, and you may not want them to know right now. However, this is a critical stage; so, you must take care of yourself. There is a lot that happens in this stage to both you and your Baby. As the parent, only you can tell.

During your first trimester of pregnancy, you may complain of fatigue, cramping, light bleeding, and are afraid to be romantic with your mate. Why am I so tired when I am not even showing yet? For all the women that have ever been pregnant, you usually can't wait to see that first little baby bump. No one will really notice it; except you and maybe your husband. (*Basically, because he knows just to go along with it)*. So, we stand in the mirror and say OMG! I'm really going to have a baby as we push our stomachs out so we can look pregnant. The doctor's description of the baby's size at this stage is comparable to the size of a kidney bean. Your budding baby's earlobes, eyelids, mouth and nose are also taking shape. What does that look like for your business? Well let's see.

You have conceived, which means:

- You know what type of business you want
- You own or have regular access to a computer and internet
- You own office supplies (just the basics)
- You have an email address
- And you're thinking about marketing ideas (website, facebook page)
- You know who or what you are targeting.

So, your Baby is budding, it is about the size of yes, a kidney bean. Even though this Baby is only the size of a kidney bean, it's your kidney bean and you love it! You're excited! You can't wait to see it in its fullness. What is it going to look like? What direction is this going to take you in life? You are excited, and yet afraid. Even though your Baby is just the size of a kidney bean, you have planned its entire future. Your Baby is going to be on Oprah Super Soul Sunday. I love it. I say, if you are going to dream, dream Big. However, let's get through this First trimester so we can tighten everything up and be ready to do just that. Let's not bleed and ignore the bleeding. Give yourself a chance to get over the morning sickness, increased urination, fatigue, dizziness, heartburn, and just plain emotions and fear. This stage can be so exciting, yet pretty exhausting. It's so easy to just want to quit, which is why I have three steps I want you to follow.

STEP 1: Jump

Step one is so simple, and I have to thank a famous comedian for reminding me to do it. He calls it **JUMP. This, is your very first step.** Let me start by saying, I love Steve Harvey, not just Steve Harvey the comedian, but also Steve Harvey the radio/Tv show host, Steve Harvey, the actor and recently Steve Harvey, the author. I have never known a black comedian who was aired on a day time talk show. I have never known a black comedian to host a major game show do you know any? I imagine that before he jumped, people asked him "Do you really think you can really accomplish all of that?" Steve has shown us that not only did he think he could do it, but that he WOULD DO IT! Yes, you can & yes, he did. Thank You Steve, for reminding us to JUMP.

I have loved watching him become successful doing something that he has always wanted to do. It's not just Steve Harvey; I love to see people succeed. I love to watch people strive for something and achieve it. It doesn't matter to me how big or small their goal is. If a person's goal is to get hired by a certain company and that's what will make them happy, then I am happy for them because that is the vision that God gave to them.

My mom had four children who graduated from college, yet she had a dream of her own. I will have to almost write another book to tell you about this amazing woman, but let me stay focused. Anyway, her dream was to get her GED. She was the daughter of a share cropper, and never got a chance to finish school. However, she wanted to go back and get her GED. We encouraged her to go back and she did just that. We were so proud of her because that was an amazing accomplishment for her and it filled our hearts with so much joy, just to watch her accomplish it.

How did a mother that did not have a high school education encourage all five of her children to go to college? Four college graduates; myself, the oldest, in Business Management, my first brother Kelvin, in Kinesiology; my middle brother, Randy in Mathematics (who majors in Mathematics on purpose?); my baby sister Angela, in Business Finance; while my baby brother Rodney received his degree in football from the NFL (he was the first-round draft pick and played for eight years). Can you believe that all of us descended from two parents who once picked cotton?

I remember one night during my last year in college; I'd come home from work and found my mom and sister in my mom's bed studying. Not a TV on, no radio, no lights except for the room they were in. I knew my sister was a nerd, but I had never seen that side of my mom. On that night, I began to understand the nerdiness and the fight that my siblings and I had all acquired. I did not know where it came from, but it was our heritage! We did not know what it meant to quit anything, it wasn't allowed in our home. I'm sure many of you can relate to this. Our parents would say, that whatever you do or whatever you become, you had to be the best at it. *Oh, my parents were at your house also?*

Then you can complete these sentences.

If you are going to be a garbage man that you'd better be the _____ that ever existed.

If you are going to be a cook you better be the _____.

If you are going to be a barber than you better be the _____.

Lol *Yass*, I bet our parents knew each other! Well, it was those statements that made us fight, and not quit. Remember though, you can't be the best, you can't fight; you can't even quit if you refuse to ***first*** JUMP!

I think part of the reason that it has taken me so long to write this book, is because I did not want to just write any kind of book. I wanted to write a book that made a difference and would help someone. No, I don't know everything. I don't even know a lot, I just know what I know. I know people, management and business. I want you to know what you know, know what you are good at and stand tall in that. As you build this business, you don't want to let this thing called fear take over.

You see, fear will cause you to do things that are out of character. Fear will make you come up with every excuse and keep you doing things that aren't even important. It's ok to be scared. Anytime you are about to JUMP, you should be shaking in your shoes, but as Steve would say, JUMP anyway. To do what you are called to do, means you must be willing to be afraid and vulnerable. The first thing you are going to do is replace Fear, with FAITH. I have faith in you because you have done so many things in your life that you did not think were even possible. You are going to dig deep to figure out WHY. Why would someone so smart and determined allow a four-letter word to stop them? I can relate because I almost let it stop me too. You will have to know what God told you to do and be ok with that. Owning a business is a huge step, and you will have many challenges. As Steve would say, your parachute will not open at first, you will need to JUMP for your parachute to open, and when you JUMP, you will have succeeded in getting some wind underneath it.

Can I say something? You need to be careful about who you surround yourself with. They don't mean any harm, but they just may not understand the dream that God gave to you. The assignment He gave you. If others understand what you are doing, then they can accept it and even encourage you. If a person can sing, people will say sing girl or sing boy. If a person can play a sport, swimming, football, etc.; they are encouraged as little children to flow in that line. If a person can play an instrument, they are encouraged because that's something most people are familiar with. However, if a person is into management or is starting a business, people don't always understand that. No, you are not just bossy, you have the gift of identifying a problem; usually before it happens, and you are trying to offset it. Frankly, it is usually seen as bossy. So, like your pregnancy, sometimes it is best to keep it to yourself while you are in the first trimester. You are already scared and questioning your own ability. You are feeling sick and constipated; all those pregnancy symptoms.

You may need to wait sometimes until you are at a stage of not turning back, before you begin to share! You need to feel better, have gotten a few things in place before you can accept the questions. You have already jumped, and in some cases, been pushed out of the plane and you do not need to be floating around in the air with stories in your head that others have put there. You know these stories, right? The stories about how difficult it is to be an entrepreneur, how most start-up businesses fail or how hard it is to work a full-time job and start a business. Get other people's stories out of your head. This is your story and you are the one who has to JUMP!

I had an associate who was wonderfully talented at her craft. She started a side business with her God-given craft and was successful at it. She became so busy that all of her down time was spent providing service to her customers. The side business was growing so fast that it began to outgrow her available time. In theory, this was no longer a side business, but she was afraid to JUMP. Instead of taking the business plan that a business associate had prepared for her to guide her into a full-time establishment, she refused to JUMP. She became afraid that the parachute wouldn't work and she retreated to her old life. She eventually stopped offering her magnificent service, even though faithful customers were regularly calling and begging for her services.

So, to my newly pregnant parents, I am so glad you decided to JUMP. Now, let's replace fear with FAITH.

Getting back to my mom, she did get her GED, and we celebrated it as if she had gotten her PhD. We got her to take a graduation picture, which hangs on her wall today with all our graduation pictures. She calls it her Wall of Fame!! That was her dream, to get her GED, and for her children to be able to take care of themselves. Mom, I hope we have all made you proud!

Now my dad; that's a horse of a totally different color. I remember the first time I ever really saw my dad angry with me. I had been teaching high school for a few years, and during the summer I had accepted a temporary job at one of the top computer companies. My car was in the shop and I asked my dad to take me to work. The computer company that everyone had been trying to get on with had offered me a full-time position, and I could not wait to share the news with my dad. So, my dad picks me up in his blue ford extended cab pickup truck, and we are riding to work. Before I could even tell him the news, he asked, "So, what are your plans?" I replied, "I'm glad you asked! This company just offed me a full-time position here and I accepted." My dad replied, with a hint of astonishment in his voice, "Why in the world would you do that?"

I was speechless, and I did not know what to say next. I thought he would be proud and excited! My next tactic, was to try to sell the company to him. I said, "Dad, are you familiar with this company? They are number one in the computer industry. Anybody that's anybody is trying to get hired there." By that time, we had pulled up near the company. I said, "Dad look at this place. It's new. It's gorgeous. It is growing. There is so much room for advancement, and they treat their employees well. And they want me!" He probably does not even remember this and I'm sure he doesn't even remember saying these words to me. He said, "*Yes Baby, but it is __not__ yours.* ……………………………….. Yes, at that point, my heart stopped beating. **It is not your Baby.**

He looked into my eyes and said, with marked intensity, "I raised you and I know what you are made of. I know the desires of your heart. I know what you are capable of. Go, start a temporary employment company. You have a good judgement of character, very good management and people skills and you can supply the temporary help that this company and other companies may need. That way, when they get paid, you get paid. You are getting a little out of everyone's pay check. Do you see what I see? *This is not yours,* and I did not pay for you to go to college to have you build someone else's business. You are my child. It took me decades to get off my job and I won't have it from you." (*Well then, he told me*). Every day after that conversation with my dad, as I walked into that building, everything looked different to me. It looked like I was in a dream, spinning around. Yes, I would still go to work every day, but I could not get that one phrase out of my head "**Yes baby, but it is not yours.**" And so, I started praying for direction. It did not take long. A few months later, I decided to open an event planning company. Stay with me. At this point, I'm newly married, maybe for about a year. I walk in and say to my husband, "Baby, I want to start my own business." He said, "OK," as he kept on shaving, never even looking up at me. I said, "however, I would like to do it full time so that I can grow it faster." He said, "OK," still not looking up at me. Ok he must be just answering me, let me take this to another level. I said, "That means I would have to quit my job." He said, "OK." .... Yes, you got it; my heart just stopped beating again. Then he spoke, "So, when are you turning in your two-week notice?" I said............. "Well, I don't know, when can I?" He said, "Tomorrow, if you like." I could not move, and I felt sick to my stomach. Then he looks up, dries his face and takes a deep breath. He looks at me and says "Listen Baby, I know who I married. I believe in you. And let's get this straight, I have not and will never require you to work. You can if you like, but if you choose not to, that just means that you will live the lifestyle that I can provide for you. So, you can turn your two-week notice in tomorrow." *Gotta Love that Man!* Right there and then, I knew I had made the right choice by marrying him. I wanted to have his babies! I turned in my notice the very next day. A week later, I went to church and told people that I had quit my job and I was about to start my own business. I was soooo excited!

One of the members overheard me and said "Why in the world would you do that? You work for one of the largest computer companies that exists. Everyone is trying to get hired by this great company!" My reply was, "You are absolutely correct, **but it's not my company**."

That was in 1990, and I have never worked for anyone else since then. Now there are two lessons in this story for you. The first, is to surround yourself with people who will encourage you to JUMP and if you don't JUMP fast enough, they will push you; assuring you that your parachute would open. Secondly, don't share your information until you are ready and confident that your parachute will open. There isn't anything wrong with working for a company; large or small. There is absolutely nothing wrong with it, but there is nothing wrong with your desire to work for yourself, either. Being an entrepreneur is my destiny, and obviously it is your destiny too. Don't allow anyone, including yourself, to make you feel bad about following your entrepreneurial spirit.

STEP 2: Kiss

Now, to the next step, which is as simple as the first: **KISS**! Yes **KISS**-KEEP IT SIMPLE AND SWEET. Ok, new expectant parents, let's not make this hard. I am not saying that there aren't a ton of things that need to be done, but they don't all have to be done today. In addition to that, remember that you do not need the top of the line everything. You do not need 1000 pamphlets, 1000 letter heads, business cards, telephone systems, custom printed ink pens, and mugs. No, at least, not yet. You will get there, however that is not something you need to start with. You do not need all brand-new, latest and greatest or the most expensive things when you only have three clients!

You can just make some of this up as you go. You can appear to be big. You can present yourself as big, especially with all of today's technology. A home-based business is very acceptable; however, your clients and customers do not have to know that you work from home, unless you want them to. They don't have to know that you are sitting in your house in your PJs, drinking a cup of coffee as you answer their calls. There is no need for them to know that you run between your office and the kitchen to make sure you are not burning dinner as you process their credit card payments. No, it's none of their business.

I have had my current homebased business for 17 years and my customers that have been with me for 17 years still don't know that I run this company from my house. They do not know that I have washed clothes, washed my children's hair, cleaned my house, watched movies, and answered their calls in my underwear. Ok, that may be a little too visual (If you've noticed, I'm quite transparent). Well, you get the point.

This is an absolute rule: Don't just Fake it until you make it. Fake it forever!

Don't worry about hiring many employees too early. Only hire who you need to be successful. For example, my sister, who was in high school at the time, helped me with my very first business. As I mentioned earlier, we were newly married, living in our first apartment, and looking for our first home. She helped me with all the clerical stuff, since I am absolutely the worst clerk.

I love organized files. I really do love order. When I ask for something, I want you to be able to produce it. I am just not capable of consistently doing this job. I am at my best with an assistant, which is exactly what she became to me. She helped me design everything. We looked back at it a couple of years later and laughed, wondering why on earth anyone hired us, but they did and that was all that mattered. I did not even buy a computer, my dad had an old one in his closet. So, my startup cost was almost zero. I had quit my job and we were trying to purchase a home; so, we were on a very tight budget. I was determined for this business to work because in the process of starting, I quickly realized that my dad was right. I loved working for myself and I was disciplined enough to do so.

So, I worked tirelessly from morning until night. I was determined to replace my salary because I did not just want us to buy a new home; I wanted to buy some new things to go inside of the home. I was facing the stark reality that My sister would be graduating from high school in a few months. Therefore, I had to find someone else to replace her.

As a high school teacher, I had taught typing and a sweet freshman named Tanya was one of my students who was very organized and an excellent typist. In fact, I would have her keep all my things organized at school, from my bulletin board to my grade book. She did it all, and I could trust that she was honest and completely dependable. In retrospect, I always knew I was going to have a business because I used to say to her, "Girl, when I start my business I'm going to hire you." and she would smile and say, "Ok Miss Hampton." (I wasn't married then.)

Well, three years later I was married, and had started my own business. My sister was moving to Washington D.C., to attend Howard University on a full scholarship (I did tell you she was a nerd right). In all honesty, my family was one which consisted of full time nerds; we all were. I love her to death. Even today they call us peanut butter and jelly mixed together, we are totally inseparable! In fact, she just finished writing her first book, which she titled "Bring out the Millionaire in You." You know I had to drop that in, right? I would not have been a good big sister and coach if I didn't. Well, back to the subject of this conversation: With Angela going off to college, I had to figure out who was I going to hire and Tanya came readily to mind. By now, she was a graduating senior, and I needed to get in touch with her ASAP, as there were only three days left in the semester.

So, I called the school where I use to teach, and had a message delivered to her. She was excited to receive my call. She was going to stay home and go to college in Houston. And so, it turned out that the plan was going to work out great for the both of us. Tanya worked for me until she graduated from college and she went on to teach school and later become an entrepreneur.

If you are an organized person, then you probably won't need a Tanya, but you may need someone else that better completes you at work; or you may not need anyone at all. Just know what and who you need, if anyone. Don't hire anyone just for the sake of hiring, or just to be able to say that you have employees. Only hire who you really need. Only hire the person that will help you to succeed.

You don't have to start with business plans; this is not to say that you will never need one. You just don't have to start with all the legal stuff completed. Once you get some clients then we can talk about what's necessary. With that completed, you can proceed to step three.

STEP 3: As Nike would say, "Just Do It"

And that's all I have to say about that!

TAKEAWAYS for You're Having A Baby:

- JUMP
- Replace Fear with Faith
- KISS (**K**eep **I**t **S**imple & **S**weet)
- Don't just fake it till you make it, fake it forever
- Just Do It!

CHAPTER 3

PREPARING YOUR HOME FOR YOUR NEW BABY

When preparing your home for your Baby, there are pros, cons and adjustments that must be made; and soon, at that. When we first started our home-based business, my husband changed to the night shift so we would have ample time to work on the business, and so he could still work at both jobs. Reggie would go to work from 10 p.m. until 6 a.m., get off work, and come home to change his clothes. At 7a.m. sharp, he would begin pickups for our home-based business. While he was doing that, I would be getting the children ready, drop them off at school, day care and do the other 100 things that I had to do. He would finish picking up; go put flyers out on doors, and when I could, I would help him; but that wasn't often. He would then come home and input all the tickets in the computer, and finally, print out the necessary paper work for the next day. Hubby would eat, then take a shower and get to bed for about three or sometimes four hours. He would get up, go pick up everything for our customers, and deliver it. He would finish at about 6p.m. The two of us had committed to marketing for two hours every day from 6:30 to 8:30p.m., and our goal was to sign up five customers every day. I would meet him to market at 6:30 and between the two of us, we would sign up our five customers. He would then get home at about 9 p.m., take another shower, and leave for work at 10 p. m. After working from 10 p.m. -6 a.m., he'd then do the same thing the next day.

My sister called him Batman! Get the joke? It was that he would slide down the pole and come out changed in the necessary uniform. I remember it like it was yesterday; he was paying the bills for the business and he said, "Baby, it just doesn't seem right to work this hard and not get paid at the end of two weeks." He was right. It absolutely didn't make sense. That is why you have got to be certain that this works for you, because start up can be a booger bear, with no paycheck at the end of two weeks. In fact, this is one of the biggest cons when you first start working for yourself. This part of being pregnant with your business can be a lot like being pregnant. Sometimes you are so tired; in the morning you have morning sickness, there are so many hormonal changes, and you are learning new things. You are learning what you are really made of. You are excited because you are realizing that you can really do this! It can be so overwhelming, but mostly, it is exciting.

Your schedule will not look like our schedule; those were goals that we set for ourselves. It worked for us, and my husband survived it all. We built the business, and it was very successful, nevertheless it was not fulfilling for my husband. You see, for my husband, our home business was just another source of income, his one true love was always Law Enforcement. I took over the business, which was my love. I hired a couple of drivers and let Reggie get back to what he really loved.

So, working from home was not for my husband and this brings me to ask you one of the most important questions to which you must figure out an answer: **Is working from home, for you?**

Working from home

I'm sure you would like to know how this works. *What is it really like? What can I expect? Can I really do this? Is it worth it?* I'm sure these, and many more questions are running through your mind as you consider starting a home-based business. Working from home, like anything else, has both pros and cons; which you should be aware of. You need to make sure that this is for you.

In my opinion, and of course, speaking from experience, one of the hardest things about working from home is people accepting the fact that you **really** work. The only way that this can be accomplished is if you set boundaries. You have to develop a schedule, and set goals that you are willing to stick to; yet be willing to break, when necessary. I know that's very oxymoronic, but I will explain it later. For now, let's just consider some of the pro and cons you can expect as your Baby grows. Well, what would you like the pros first, or the cons? Fine, we'll start with the pros.

Pros: Working from home has so many advantages, like right now, I have food cooking and a load of clothes washing. I have on a wrinkled t-shirt, wrinkled work out pants, socks with flip flops, and my hair is in a rubber band; all while writing this book. I have my cell phone next to me in case someone calls me from my office. Oh, *I'm sorry, hold on a minute, guys…………………… Ok, I'm back, that was my dentist's office calling to inform me that my crown is in, and to confirm that they could do both appointments on the same day. Yes, this is really happening as I am writing this chapter.*

I'm not being deceiving when I say there are advantages to working from home. Although, I'd like to let you know that the events of this day are not a norm for me. It is not normal for me to walk around the house looking such a mess. Anyone who knows me and is reading this probably can't even imagine my description of myself. My routine is that each day I wake up, I have my quiet time in the morning, then workout, shower, put on some everyday make up, get completely dressed so that anytime I need to leave the house I am ready to go. In fact, I did not get dressed on purpose, so it would make me stay home and write for you today. The only way I could make myself stay home was to put on something that I would not want to be seen out in. Back to the pros.

Well, some of the pros are financial savings on minor expenses like your dry-cleaning and lunch, more time with your children, flexibility, having time to cook and much more. If you have been dry cleaning your clothes for work, you will see a huge savings in this area, now that you're working from home. Another area is lunch. Have you ever processed how much money you spend on lunch? American workers spend an alarmingly high amount of their hard-earned cash on somewhat average daily expenses, according to a new Workonomix survey by Accounting Principals. The survey found that 50 percent of the American workforce spends approximately $1000 a year on coffee, or a weekly coffee habit of more than $20. And the spending doesn't even stop there.

Two thirds (66 percent) of working Americans buy their lunch instead of packing it, costing them an average of $37 per week — nearly $2,000 a year. We are not even going to talk about breakfast meal and snacks, chips at work, cookies, office parties, sodas, etc. Well you get the point. You will save money in this area and you become very protective of all those left-over meals. Until I began working from home, I would easily dispose of one small piece of chicken, a single spoonful of green beans, or a few potatoes. Now, as I clean the kitchen, I am scraping the pots from today's dinner, to create tomorrow's lunch for myself. Instead of chips and soda, I may grab a hand full of grapes, a bowl of cheerios, an apple or pop-corn. The dollars that I would have put into a vending machine are no more. Besides, there is no vending machine around.

Some of the other visible advantages include being at home when my children were sick and being able to get a doctor's appointment in the middle of the day. When you work from home, you are not so stressed about what time you can or cannot go to the doctor or dentist. Do you remember the phone call that interrupted us earlier? I wanted an appointment, so I would not have to go to the dentist twice. Since I was flexible, I was not only able to get the appointments together, I was able to get an appointment one week earlier. This is what I was talking about earlier when I said you need to have a schedule and stick to it; but at the same time break it. This also goes for lunch. Since you work from home, you don't have much interaction with people as often as most other people, so when a friend is trying to go to breakfast or lunch, I rearrange my day so I can laugh and talk with other people face to face; instead of on the phone.

Now I need to be clear about this: this cannot be your norm or you will never get anything done. You will have to learn how to say "No, not today," but that's in the next chapter. Are we clear?

Ok, now, where were we? I just remembered an interesting observation I've noticed over the years: You will soon notice how many people are at home during the day! When I first started working from home, I was amazed. I'm sorry this absolutely had nothing to do with our conversation, but please, just stay with me. We're still on those pros; aren't we? Other advantages are being able to cook, clean, and work; all at the same time. I typically set my alarm clock to remind me to stop working and start cooking. I don't know about you, but I can cook a meal in about 30 minutes. Oh, I don't call my office the house, it's my office. So, I would run in the house, cook, and then go back to my office. My goal would be to have food completed by a certain time.

There were certain other pros such as, I could make it to earlier classes for the extra-curricular activities with my children. If I was still working for someone else, I would not have gotten off work until 5p.m.! Therefore, I could not book a gymnastic class for 4p.m. I discovered that the 4p.m. class was not as crowded, because most parents are still at work and bring their children to the 5p.m. class. And a helpful hint for those of you with young children, the children in the early classes received lots of extra attention!

And what about traffic. Have you ever sat in bumper-to-bumper traffic silently cursing? Or maybe not so silently? I usually don't book any appointments before 10a.m. or 10:30a.m. I do this so I can let people get where they are going. I feel like I am in the way of others when I am out too early. They have their routine in place and because I am working from home I feel like maybe I am slowing them down or not respecting them by being on the streets. There are enough cars out there. So, again, you should also save on gas and mileage. Well, the truth is I haven't always found that to be true for me, because I like to roam. Even at night, I was good for just taking a ride. My husband would always wonder how someone who works from home puts so many miles on a car.

As you can see, there are many advantages to working from home, way too many to even talk about. These are just the ones that easily come to mind. I could go on and on about the pros, however, let's discuss some of the things that might trip you up by working from home.

Cons

Irrespective of the above listed pros, there are also many cons about working from home, and I will list a few, then talk a little bit about them.

- Flexibility
- Distractions
- No Drama
- No sick days
- Hats
- House work

Flexibility

Working from home takes a lot of discipline. The truth is that while you can do whatever you like, it can become a double-edged sword, (i.e. your flexibility **isn't necessarily a positive thing**). You must be very careful because you are the only person who can decide if your flexibility will be a consistently positive thing. Initially, you will start making all types of adjustments to your schedule to help others. People will see that you are dressed comfortably and appear to be available. But you are NOT available. The first thing you must do is discipline yourself to get up. Yes, get out of the bed. And you must discipline yourself to stick to today's plans. Go to bed every night knowing what your tomorrow will look like. If you have no idea where you are headed, then you can absolutely be guided in any direction. Family, friends and neighbors will ask, "can you drop me off here?"; "Will you take me to get my car?"; or "Let's go to lunch." If your response is always yes, you can and will become very distracted; all because you are not in control. However, for this to work, you must be in control; you must have goals and stick to them with tenacity.

Yes, flexibility can be a double-edged sword, which is why I have it listed both with the pros and the cons. Flexibility is awesome if you have it under control and don't allow it to control you. However, if you don't get this under control early, you will end up having major problems. Then there is the distraction of social media, telephone, and TV, which are only a few that quickly come to mind.

Distractions

Let us start with social media. Have you ever gotten on social media (e.g. Instagram, Facebook) to look up one thing and an hour later you are still on there, worse still, you haven't done what you went on social media to do? Instead, you have been watching videos, liking pictures, typing birthday wishes, looking up recipes, (as if you are going to use them!), looking up pictures, or whatever. That index finger is just swiping that screen up and down and tapping on everything. You have been letting this little device steal your time! Well, you are not alone, and knowing and accepting this is the very first step.

It's like AA. Hello, my name is DEBBIE and I am addicted to social media. Give yourself a timeline. For me I don't even allow myself to get on social media in the morning because I alarmingly went from never being on social media, to it taking over my entire day. I would get on social media before I had my quiet time, before I even got out of the bed! It would cause me to start my day late, and ultimately, have me rushing to meetings. I became really alarmed because my lifestyle wasn't one of rushing. I don't rush, I plan. It is a fun and informative distraction. I don't know how in the world teachers are able to teach these days, because if we as adults are having this problem, I can't begin to imagine how the poor children are managing.

Then there is the TV. I know you have not been home, so you may not know how this box can steal your time. You may just start off with watching the news, just having the tv on for company, just to have some noise in the house, but, before you know it you have gotten pulled into a show that you don't even like. Then of course, you need to watch tomorrow to see who going to be on, who's better, and so you can get the outcome of what you are watching today. Before you know it, you will have a regular tv schedule. And let's not even begin to talk about watching what we have taped. That can easily turn into two hours. So, for me and my house; I don't even turn it on during the day. I play music, and during the holidays I turn the tv on to the holiday music channel.

Now let me tell you why that is even dangerous for me. Because I love, love, love all Christmas movies. Especially the Hallmark ones. Did I say love? I mean LOVE them. My daughter always says, "Mom, I don't know how you watch these, they all end the same way." I think I just like the simplicity of them. In addition, everyone usually gets what they want and I love that. Consequently, from Thanksgiving to New Year's I listen to Christmas music and watch Christmas movies. I tape them so that at night and on the weekends, all throughout the holidays, I have a list of Christmas movies to watch. Anyway, now you get the point. Turn the tv off, play some music and get your butt to work.

No Drama

One of the biggest pros and cons about working from home is there is no drama. Now, I was never into drama, however, working from home can be "drama boring." Yes, I just made that phrase up. You do not even get the opportunity to overhear a conversation until you get a few employees. So, I tape and watch one reality show. My husband would come in and say I can't believe you are watching this and I would say hey, I do not have any drama in my life and though I love it that way, there's that little part of me that just wants to hear a little something. *Oh whatever, I know I'm not alone.* God is not through with me yet (That's what we always say when we know better and can't come up with anything else)!

I watch one housewives show, and the truth is, I have a love/hate relationship with it. I tried to add another, but thank God, I quickly realized that one was enough. I think this is how stay at home moms become hooked on soap operas. I get it now. To be honest though, as your Baby grows, you will not have time for tv, social media, or anything else. When you have nothing to do, even though I don't know when that is, you want to do just that. NOTHING. SLEEP.

No Sick Days

Now let's talk about sick days. There aren't any. You are it. You can call in if you want to, just know what that does to your tomorrow and the next day. If you are ok with that, "call in" to yourself. This is probably one of the hardest adjustments when you first start a business. Working, being sick and not getting paid. I remember Oprah talking about how she did her show for 25 years, and never called in sick. She talked about how she has worked under every condition. She said that she just could not do it. Guests would have planned to be there to meet her. Many of them had taken off work, flew all the way there to meet and see her in person and she just could not let them down. She talked about how she has worked while harboring various sicknesses, but in 25 years she never called in. While viewing the last taping of her show, I gained a new-found respect for her. I had always loved Oprah, but I had never stopped to give her daily appearance, with "no sick days" any thought.

Now we all know that Oprah had a large staff, but none of them were OPRAH. If you had tickets to see Oprah, that's who you wanted to see. As much as we like her best friend Gayle; that is not who we would have come to see, I would have loved meeting Gayle but that would have been extra. We came to see Oprah. This is Oprah, there is no replacement for her. She can have hundreds of employees, Gayle, Stedman, executive producers, famous guests, etc. This is Oprah & You are YOU!!! There is no one to replace you either, so show up every day with everything you have in you.

Hats

There is only one Oprah and guess what? There is only one YOU! When you own a home-based business, you are the accounting department, you are the answering service, you are the computer repair person; you wear all hats. Tag, you are it. Get sick if you must Missy; but you are still it! Do you get it? That's why we want to grow your Baby up as quickly as possible so that it won't be completely dependent on you.

The day finally came where I could take time off, and I now have such a well-oiled machine, that I can write a book while running a home-based business. For me, it's finally time to implement yet another business, since my grown Baby is not as dependent on me anymore. This day will arrive for you too. I am going to help with this process so you can move a little quicker and more smoothly; without losing yourself and your family.

Housework

And then there is the house work. Is it ever all done? No, so let us decide what we are going to do and stick with that. Other things will come up with the house. Repairs and renovations will be needed and service people will come while you are home. You are it, so you must take care and balance. Right now, in this stage there is not another you. Let me ring that loud and clear: THERE IS NOT ANOTHER YOU! We are going to fix this, but not at this stage. You are Oprah; you are the O factor. You are the most important thing to your Baby so let's keep that in mind.

For me, working at home has been a wonderful experience. At this point in my life, I would not be able to be up, dressed and arrive on time to a job, on a daily basis. I don't think, let me correct that, I know that I would not be a good employee to anyone else. I am glad that my dad reminded me of who I was meant to be. People go a life time knowing that they are supposed to be doing something else; yet are so afraid to JUMP and take that chance.

It is something you should not let me or anyone else talk you into. It must be your decision. It must be your desire. Remember, you can't call in sick, you are 'it'. Even when you are sick, tag you are "it." I did have to make some sacrifices early on, however, I would not change a thing. I have been able to balance it all; my business, employees, marriage, and children. This is just a glimpse of life working from home. Now that I have finished this chapter, I am going to go put on some real clothes, comb my hair, and get out of this house for a few hours. It is beautiful outside! It is in the mid 70's sunny with a little breeze. TTYL (Talk to you later).

TAKEAWAYS for Preparing Your Home for Your New Baby:

- Is working from home really for you?
- Set clear goals and boundaries that are realistic for you
- Flexibility is a double-edged sword
- Don't rush, instead plan
- Tag, you are IT. In the beginning, you are IT

SECOND
TRIMESTER

CHAPTER 4
NO IS A NICE WORD

Congratulations, you've made it to your second trimester. You know what to expect, you've started preparing and are well aware of the pros and cons of having your Baby. Now, just like a regular pregnancy, patience and tenacity are required to get you through this trimester. Just because you are feeling better, does not mean that you try to do everything. This is the stage where I get to teach you that NO is a nice word.

People might not always like the word NO; but it is a nice word and they will learn to absolutely respect it. As an entrepreneur, you will be required to say no to clients, vendors, suppliers, employees, family, friends, and even yourself. People often say "yes" to things they don't want to do, simply because they don't want to appear to be mean or uncaring. Saying NO is not something that comes naturally to most people, says Susan Newman, PhD, social psychologist and author of The Book of No. Newman adds, "For some, saying 'yes'; agreeing to take on whatever is asked of them has become an addiction. Our lack of ability to say 'no' isn't a personal flaw we're born with—saying 'no' is a learned behavior. As we continue to grow, we are rightfully encouraged to be nurturing and caring and that usually involves agreeing to help others or saying 'yes' to their whims and desires. By the time we reach adulthood, it's no wonder most of us suffer anxiety at just the thought of saying 'no' to someone.

I'm extremely grateful to my mom for helping me master the art of saying no without any anxiety a long, long time ago. You know how it is when you are growing up and you ask your mom for something and she says NO. Then you begin begging and pleading "Mom please, please, please Mom. Why? I don't understand why I can't I have this or why can't I do that." You would beg and plead until you wear your mom out. Not my mom. Her NO meant NO.

I remember when I was in high school I wanted to go to this party so bad. I did all the things a teenager should do to put your parents in a good mood before you ask the big question. I cleaned my room and did any extra chores that needed to be done. And then I went to my mom and said "Mom, I am going to ask you something but I don't want you to answer me right now. I don't care what the answer is, even if it is yes don't answer me, just hear me out." Then I proceeded, "There is a party Friday after the football game. Now, I know our games are over a little late but Mom, this is like the party of the year and I really, really, really want to go. I know how you feel about late parties but I just want you to know how important this is and I really, really, really want to go. Don't answer yet mom, just hold your peace."

You see, my mom's NO meant NO. If she said maybe, it could go either way; it meant she probably just needed more information. Or Mom's maybe meant that if you said the right things you could possibly convince her. But if Mom said NO… NO meant NO. For this party, I could not take that chance. I had to hold on to the possibility of attending; at least a few more days. I said, "I will check back with you on Wednesday, but please don't answer me before then." She said "Okay." Now, to this day, I don't remember if I was able to attend that party or not, but what I do remember is that I could not and would not let that lady get NO out of her mouth; because when NO came out, there was no changing her mind. In fact, if you would try and change my mom's mind you would get in trouble and there could be additional punishment. She would say something like "Not only can you not go this time, but don't ask me next week either. When I say, NO I mean NO. And you know how sometimes parents give in, if you have your friends to ask? In our house that was almost an automatic NO. In her nicest and sweetest voice, Mom would say to the friend "NO, baby she cannot go." Then she would come into the house or get into the car and very sternly say "When I tell you NO, I mean NO. Don't have your friends to call or come and ask, do not have anyone's mom or dad to call me. There is no need for the teacher, the preacher or anyone else to ask. This is my house. You are my child and when I say NO, I mean NO!" *(Really mom, the teacher and preacher?)*. You did not have to put them in this. Lol.

Now, it seemed like my mom said no to a lot of things, but if you really wanted to do something, you had to learn to start with "Mom, I'm going to ask you something but please don't answer me right now." I watched this go on and on down the line for all five of us. When the younger ones were learning this, and would start to whine/beg we would say "Noooo, you don't want to do that. Whining and begging is a guaranteed NO.

How is NO a nice word, you ask? Well it lets people know where you stand. My mom had that down all too well. As I got older, I realized that I had learned to say NO without it being a problem. I also had the utmost respect for the word NO and the person that could deliver it. It was a matter of respect. It does not lead you on. It was just NO. Have you ever had someone tell you that they were going to do something and they didn't? Oooh!! Doesn't that make you mad! Don't you wish that they would have just said NO, so you could have gone to do something else or made other plans? NO isn't a word that people like, but they respect it. When you say NO, it says to a person, I respect you and your time.

41

Most people think that you must be mad when you say NO. Nonetheless, as I always tell people, say it with a smile. But just say it. "NO" is a nice word, but because most people are afraid to use it, when you hear it, it doesn't sound good. Now let me stress this point. Don't just say NO, just to say it. Get all the facts first. That is something that my mom always did. In fact, 95% of the time, Mom's first answer was maybe, not NO. It gave her an out. It gave her time to think about it and to hear us out. Whenever she used the word NO, she knew that without a doubt in her mind that was not happening. It was NO.

I remember one day while we were at church, and my brother Kelvin was trying to get me to take on another project and I said NO. He said, "Do you say NO to everything now? I want my sister back. Where did she go?" He was used to me being able to help and he knew I genuinely did not mind, but life had changed for me and I was so glad that my mom had taught me how to say NO. At that time, I was running my home-based business that had grown by leaps and bounds. I was also managing my youngest brother's company in Louisiana, remotely from Houston, Texas. I also had two active girls, who, by the way, were no longer in elementary, but were now involved in competitive cheer at the gym, and in addition to that, one was in the band while the other was playing volleyball. My home was the hang out house for both of their friends, and we often travelled for cheer competition. At this time, my husband was also working on his Master's degree and we were both actively helping our best friends start a new church. I had nothing left to give to anyone else. Therefore, I had to smile, and say "NO, I cannot take on anything else. When I get home, I am still Mom, I am still a wife and I am still a person." I smiled and said, "So, the answer is NO."

You know what I realized? The word NO has never killed anyone. The word NO is a two-letter word that makes a complete sentence. Let's try it. NO. See? It stands alone, and graciously at that. There is nothing needed before it or after it to understand its meaning. Just NO. I knew that I had more on my plate than I needed and it was no one's fault but mine. Sometimes, life happens. I had always run my home-based business and managed my brother's company. Now the change was with my children growing up and getting involved in everything while my husband was back in school. Well, nothing had really changed, and yet, everything had changed. My life phase had changed, and the truth is, we are all required to adapt to where we are in life. Once you have had your Baby, you must leave room for things to go wrong. You must factor in the time that you would require changing a diaper, feed your Baby or just enjoy having a Baby. If you stretch yourself too thin, then you won't have time for yourself and you can often end up not doing your best at what you have taken on.

People might not always like the word NO; but it is a nice word and they will learn to absolutely respect it. I was asked by my daughters' principal to attend a quarterly meeting as the liaison officer for their school. She tried to sell the position by saying that meetings were scheduled for only once a quarter, and that she thought I would be great at this. You know what my reply was? I said, "Miss, thank you so much for thinking of me but I am going to have to decline. I have quite a bit on my plate right now and I don't want to tell you that I am going to do something and not be able to do it. I think it would be best if you find someone else." Now didn't I just say NO? She went on convincingly to say "Mrs. Porter, it's only once a quarter, and it absolutely requires no work, on your part. You are just there to represent our school, and I know you would be great at it." Again, I replied, "Oh, you are so kind, but I am still going to have to decline. Thank you so much for thinking of me and I am sure that you will find someone that is eager to help you out." (Saying NO with a smile is such a great concept!) I could have accepted the position and one day, the quarterly meeting could have fallen on a day that I needed to be out of town or on payroll day at the office. First, let me back up. I **Hate** meetings. They are necessary, but are usually too long and we drag them out. This usually happens because we are trying to coerce people into agreeing with us and often there are no real objectives or timetables for meetings. The sooner you put it out there, the quicker everyone can say yes or NO, and move on. That is why I Love the "One Minute Manager". I require all my managers to not just read it, but to implement it. Don't let anyone talk you into doing things that you don't want to do. I am sure the principal did not like the fact that I said NO; however, she really would not have liked it if I had accepted the position and not attended the meeting, or had been ineffective at the position.

What is the lesson here? Let your NO, be NO. Now that we agree that it's okay to say NO, I want to move on to an equally interesting concept, which is *Know when you are being told NO.* Most people do not use the word NO. This is how you can determine if you are being told NO:

- If they say anything other than yes, that's usually NO.
- If they don't answer, that's usually NO. (Yes, that's correct, silence usually means NO).

Remember, people don't have a problem saying yes; they just have a problem saying NO. So, if they say, "Ok, well let me check on that." it's usually a NO. If they say, "That sounds like something I might be interested in, but let me check." It's usually a NO. If they say, "I really want to come but…" it's usually a NO.

Again, if they say nothing. It's usually a NO. This is something I had to teach my daughter. We could be standing there together talking to someone and when we finished she would say, "Oh mom, I'm so excited! She's going to do it." Then I would say, "No baby, she's not." She would happily reply, "Yes, she is! She said she really wants to, she just needs to check her schedule." I'd say, "That's a NO, baby. Remember, "Really want to, but' is a NO." I had to teach her that if a person says anything other than yes, it is usually a NO.

If you want to have a successful home-based business, you must know when you are being told NO. It will save you a lot of time, money and heartache. You not only need to know when you are being told NO, but you also need to be ok with it. You should appreciate that the person who said NO, had enough respect for you, not to waste your time or your energy. The person who tells you NO, avoids leaving you hoping, wishing and waiting.

Listen:

I want you to take the time to listen to how people say NO or should I say, how they do not say NO. Listen to yourself, and to others. Listen when a person attempts to tell you NO. There is always a lot of preliminary talk, but not with the word yes. Yes, is just, yes, and it's delivered with enthusiasm and excitement. My daughter will now walk away from a conversation and say, "Mom they said NO." I smile and reply, "Thumbs up, you're becoming a very smart girl! You are getting it."

I thank my mom with all my heart for teaching this to us early. Even though I did not like it back then, today, I absolutely emulate her. When my children were small and asked, "Mom, can we go to Chuck E. Cheese tomorrow?" I would say maybe, we'll see, or let me think about it. You know what amuses me? Now, my daughter comes to me and says something along the lines of "Mom, I'm going to ask you something, but don't answer me now." Funny, right!!

The point is, when you have a home-based business you must always leave yourself an out. Remember that you are Oprah! I never wanted to be the mom that disappointed my children. I always wanted my word to be good. If I told them that I was going to do something, I wanted them to know that they could depend on me to do just that. I want my clients or anyone else that I deal with to know that my word is good. If I tell you I am going to do something, you can take it to the bank. I want my word to be good. I want you to be able to say to anyone that questions my word, if she told you she would, then you can trust that she will. Our word is all that we have. Don't allow the fact that you can't deliver that little word NO to mess up your reputation!

Practice using the word NO today. Do you promise that you will? Practice saying NO, with a smile. Remember that saying NO never killed anyone, that I know of. Remember, NO is a nice word!

TAKEAWAYS for NO is a Nice Word:

- NO means NO
- Hear all the information before saying NO
- Say NO with a smile
- Read the One Minute Manager by Kenneth Blanchard
- Know when you are being told NO

CHAPTER 5
THE ANNOUNCEMENT

M any pregnant women decide early on that they will wait until they reach the second trimester before they will share the good news with family and friends. This trimester is often called the "honeymoon period" for good reason. Typically, the nausea has subsided, emotions have evened out and the sex drive has returned. It's also the time when you'll start to feel the baby's first movements.

Let me translate that to you. At this point in the early second trimester a woman is hitting her stride. In business, she sees signs of early success; solid routines are in place and are functioning properly. You have your office set up and you are no longer working around the clock; so to speak. You have gotten a few clients and you can see that your business is functional. Now it's time to really make the Announcement. You have put the necessary pieces in place to take on a little more. Some people may have already noticed a change in you. This is the stage that you should push a little harder, as you continue to make your dream a reality. You have worked like a crazy person and you have come to learn a lot about yourself. Tell everyone. Make the announcement. This is exciting!

At this stage, you must work with what you have and who you are. Are you a Doer or a Delegator? I am not saying that one is better than the other. I am just sincerely asking which one are you? You need to know this about yourself, so let's figure it out.

Doers

A doer is that person who actively does things instead of just thinking or talking about them. A doer gets things done. Obviously. This can be very helpful when you first start your business because there are certain things that you will have to do on your own.

Let me stop here and be perfectly honest with you. I am such a Delegator, that I am struggling with this part of my book. I love doers, without them I would not successfully get anything done because I am such a delegator. I just had to be honest and put that out there because my fingers were not moving as fast as they had been. In the beginning, I shared with you how when my sister went off to college, I was desperately looking for Tanya, the young lady that was in my typing class. That's because I know, absolutely know, within every fiber of my being, that I am a delegator. I depend on the doer to carry out my vision. I am the big picture person. The thought of starting a business without someone to pass things off to would have been totally unrealistic for me. So, the first day that I walked into my office, Tanya walked in with me. That's because I knew me. I knew what I was capable of doing and what I was not capable of doing. People will say to me "You are good at everything." My reply is "No, I just only do what I'm good at. I look for people that are better than I am in areas where I am weak. They just make me look good."

Doers are so needed, and useful; that nothing is ever going to happen without them. They are actually going to take what you have envisioned and help make it into a reality. Doers are so awesome! They are both thinkers and very talented. Doers are often excellent multi-taskers. The problem is they often overextend themselves, because they need to "do it". They may be working on small tasks but by the time they accept several small tasks, it becomes too much for one person. The doer will not stop until all tasks are completed, and while this is an impressive virtue, it is also very dangerous. Doers must have deadlines and they will consistently exceed your expectations when you follow up on their progress. Doers are perfect at taking the vision to another level. They can execute a vision, masterfully.

To be honest, we all have a little doer in us. If not, you would not be at this stage of your business. You made a decision to start your business, and to this point you have had to do things that you did not think you would ever have to do. The doer in you had to rise to the occasion. It was in you, and you had to stop talking about it and simply do it. Pat yourself on the back.

When I told my brothers, Kelvin and Randy, I was writing a book they both asked, "What made you want to write a book?' I said "I had always planned to write a book. I always knew I was supposed to." After my daughters went away to college, my sister Angie and I discussed goals we had not yet accomplished, but had always planned to accomplish together. Those goals included:

1. Write a book
2. Pledge Delta Sigma Theta
3. Learn to speak Spanish

We both had college kids and now had extra time to pursue NEW dreams. We agreed that we would start with writing a book. That was in September 2016 and now I'm writing this book in April 2017.

Let me back up and say, for at least 20 of the 28 years that I have been married, my husband would always ask "When are you going to write your book?" One of my very best friends, Sherry who is more like a sister, used to ask me the same question, for roughly the same number of years my husband has asked. She would say, "Porter, when are you going to write that book?" I call her after I finish writing each chapter and read it to her. Anyway, it was in September that my sister and I finally discussed writing our books. In October, we did nothing about it; November nothing, and you know why nothing happened in those months? It was because we did not have a plan of action, no goals set. In December we attended a seminar, signed up with a coach and guess what? She finished writing her book in February and I, finished mine in April. Therefore, I would always highlight the fact that who you hang around does matter! Who is holding you accountable? Do you know where you are headed? It is definitely important to have goals. But every goal must have deadlines! If not, your goals are just dreams.

Once you have goals and you work with a team, the next right step is to simply follow the leader. For instance, with me and my sister, sometimes I lead while she follows and sometimes she leads while I follow. Most of the time I delegate, while she's the doer. On other occasions, she delegates and I'm the doer.

Delegators

Now let's talk about Delegating for a bit. Even if you are a doer, in business you must learn to delegate, in order to grow. If not, you will get bogged down by your everyday responsibilities and you will eventually stop growing. To help your Baby grow, you must take the time to eat your veggies and take care of yourself. Sit down and think about your plans.

Yes, I am a delegator; which means that when I have a vision, I see it. My first home-based business was event planning. Even now, when I plan an event, I go through the event over and over in my head. Each time I go through it, I see it. I see how it can be improved. I see what mistakes could possibly be made, and I see how it can be better. The problem is I must remember to convey my vision to the doer because I only see it; while the doer must do it. In my sleep, I envision what the project will look like. I mean I can really see everything about it in detail. I am at the event so much that I can feel the energy. However, to pull it off, I need the doer to help make my dream a reality. I need someone who is better than I am in this area. I don't mind helping, I will often check in with the doer to make sure that they are not overwhelmed. You must get some of these things off your plate.

So, let's look at what can you delegate. I know that these things may not take long to do, but remember that you don't want a lot of tiny things to become overwhelming and hence, stunt your growth. If you're not an accountant, consider delegating payroll. There are companies that specialize in processing payroll for small companies. You should also consider setting your bills on auto pay.

When I started my current home-based business, what I absolutely needed to do was hire a driver. Yes, I could have driven; but I wanted to grow the business a little more and you usually cannot do both. The other reason is that driving is not what I do. As a matter of fact, if I had to be the driver, our business would not have lasted any time. Listen, you need to know what you can do consistently. You need to sit still and see where you are going. If you have young children you might want to hire a high school baby sitter to take some of the pressure off you. You can hire a maid to help clean your house, and if you cannot afford one bi-weekly, have one come in at least once a month. Trust me, this will relieve a lot of pressure from you.

Have you ever come home to a house that you did not clean? It is a little bit of heaven! You don't usually mind spending money on eating out, snacks, coffee, soda, etc. Give up something and get your house professionally cleaned. I will give up getting my nails done to pay that money towards a cleaning service. Now, I'm not willing to give up my pedicure. Pretty feet are mandatory for me. But I will choose a cleaning service every time; over a manicure. What small treat can you give up so that you can treat yourself to coming home to a clean home, that you didn't have to clean? Once we were trying to trim our family budget, and my husband said, "We can get rid of Vonda, our cleaning lady." After all of these years, he still hadn't gotten it. I said to him, very factually "Baby, Vonda is for you. Vonda is your best friend, and I don't think you want to get rid of her. Vonda keeps me from having a headache at night." Let's just say Vonda became a priority.

If you have children, get them involved. Kids love a new Baby. They can fold brochures, stuff envelopes, staple papers or something. A seven-year-old, in this day and age, is more advanced with technology than we are. Let them help and pay them something. Allow them to be a part of the business. And whoever you allow to help you, make it obvious that if they make mistakes, it's ok with you. Don't make it so serious, have some fun! You are going to make mistakes, and so are the people that work for you. You all are making this up together. When a mistake is made, just say "That's ok, now we know not to do that again." And simply, start over. It is important for you and the people around you not to be so tense and so serious. Enjoy this moment, as it is an exciting phase of life.

Once you hire employees it is time for more adjustments. People naturally do not like change, and it's ironic that most of the time, change is an attempt to improve! You won't know if the improvement will work unless you try it. If it doesn't work, then you can throw it out and try something else. For most people, change is hard at every phase of life. They are just so used to doing things the way that is familiar to them. My husband likes routine, while I am just the opposite, and like change. I always tell him that I know what he is doing and I usually know what time he is doing it. I love this about him, seeing as it makes him so dependable and he never forgets things, as I do. When he goes to his car he does not have to come back in the house two or three times, like I do. However, as routine as he is, he is still the relatively spontaneous one. He will just come in and say "Hey, let's go to Galveston, or let's go take a ride on the boat." I will instantly reply, "Well, I did not plan to do that…" because even though I'm not the one who has routines, I am the one that likes to have a plan. However, I admit that some of our best staycations have been the spontaneous ones that he insisted we take.

The truth is I have always been the family planner, it just made sense, that's what I did for a living. Whenever we had to go on a trip or we had an event, I was usually the planner, therefore my husband would know most of the details simply by being around when I was making those plans. A hilarious example is our annual family vacation. Every year, my mom, all my siblings, our spouses, and our children, take a vacation together; it's usually about 25 to 30 of us. About seven years ago, I passed the vacation planning torch to my sister-in-law Detra. The first year she took over, we went to New York and my husband kept asking me about the de- tails. I would say, "I don't know baby, ask Detra." When we got to the airport, he asked if we were all sitting together. I said, "I don't know baby, ask Detra." He asked how we were getting to the hotel from the airport, and I said, "I don't know baby, ask Detra." When we got to the hotel, he asked, "Are we all on the same floor?" My reply, "I don't know, ask Detra." (if you notice I have now dropped the baby). He then asked, "Hey baby, what are we doing after we check in?" I couldn't take it anymore, so I took my husband by the hand and guided him over to my sister in law and said "Reginald this is Detra, Detra this is Reginald. Reginald, Detra has the answers to all your questions. I don't know and I am enjoying not knowing, I am going to do whatever she tells me to do. I am going to stand here until she tells me what to do next." She laughed and gave him a little insight once she realized that he was going through the withdrawal phase of not knowing the details.

The lesson is this: When you delegate or turn something over let them have it. You will be amazed as to what a relief that can be. When you release it to someone, expect a wonderful outcome because you probably would not have given it to them if you did not think they could handle it.

We have been on vacation every year since. Each time, Detra has managed to outdo herself. I know what you are thinking. What family goes on vacation together with spouses, in-laws and children? We do, and it works for us. As a matter of fact, we look forward to it. We know how to stay in our lane and do what we are told by whoever may be giving the orders at that time. Usually orders come from either of my sisters-in-law, Detra or Stacie, who addresses us as "you people" when we get on her nerves. Lol. I hate to even use the word sister in law on both sides of my family because they are really my sisters. Don't tell them I said that (especially the one that calls us "you people").

By now, you must have gotten the point. To succeed, you need both the doer and the delegator. You need to be a leader, as well as a follower. You should know your strengths; and the difference between something you CAN do yourself, and something you SHOULD do yourself, and something ONLY YOU can do. This is also hard for new entrepreneurs (or even new managers) to learn. Ultimately, you might need the help of someone to help you bring your dreams into fruition.

For me, this is one thing I have learned: I need all the doers I can get, to help me make my dream a reality.

TAKEAWAYS for The Announcement:

- Set goals with deadlines, otherwise you're just dreaming
- Determine if you are a Doer or a Delegator
- Decide what you can delegate so you are not doing too much
- Let mistakes be okay and don't take yourself too seriously
- Delegators, make sure you have a doer
- Doers, make sure you have a Delegator/Manager
- Once you delegate something, let it go

CHAPTER 6

YOU ARE A WIZ AT THIS PREGNANCY THING

During the second trimester, your Baby is growing very rapidly. Although you feel much better, substantial changes are still taking place with your Baby, and one of the biggest changes is growth. My advice to you, once again, is not to take anything too seriously. Don't take yourself so seriously. Enjoy this phase. This is the time that when you look back, you will feel compelled to talk about. Like, 'I remember when...' You know how you sit around the table and talk about the good old days? Well, you are living in them. These, are the good old days! This is an exciting time in your life. Surely you have heard the saying, laughter is good for the soul. This is such a true saying.

When I started my event planning business, I made all sorts of mistakes. Although I thought I knew what I was doing, I had no idea what I was REALLY doing. However, before I knew it, I was a Wiz at it. When I looked up the definition of Wiz; it is defined as someone who has dazzling skills in any field. A Wizard is someone who is very good at something. In effect, a skilled or very clever person.

One of my favorite movies is the Wizard of Oz. To tell the truth, I can watch any version of the Wizard of Oz at any time. It can be in cartoon form, condensed version, an extended version, it doesn't really matter to me; I just love the movie. Although I can watch any version of it, I do have a favorite. My favorite version of this movie is the Wiz. Why, you ask? Because in the Wiz, I have my favorite movie and my favorite entertainer of all time, Michael Jackson, as the scarecrow. It doesn't get any better than that. Who is lucky enough to fall in love with a movie as a child and later in life, have their favorite entertainer star in it? You see, Michael Jackson and I go way back, we literally grew up together. I went to my very first concert when I was in the 3rd grade and yes, it was the Jackson 5. My cousin Gwen and I would go to see the Jackson Five every time they came to town. I remember that after the concert, I would not be able to sleep. I would be on such a high. I would dream about the concert over and over and over. You have probably experienced this with your business. I am sure that you are dreaming about it and yes, you should be. I am sure you are dreaming about what it is going to look like a year from now. How big will it be? How will it change your life for the better? Those are the dreams you should be dreaming. You must see the growth of your Baby and dream big. You must see it to believe it. I love Michael Jackson and the Wiz because it reminds me of things that must be done, as the Baby is growing. Dorothy and her friends go see the Wizard, someone who has the ability to help them. There are witches and crows to try and frighten them so they will quit; and remain where they are. Well, you will have those also. They are there to try and take over your mind and tell you that you can't win. That there are enough businesses out there providing the exact same service you claim to be providing; possibly doing it better than you are. Your witches and crows may appear in different forms.

Beware, when you are being told you can't win, because you can, and you most certainly will! There will be many of them telling you that you can't. You just need to remind yourself that you can do this.

If you are fortunate, you will have at least one other person to point you in the right direction. They will tell you to just follow the yellow brick road and ease on down the road. Please DO NOT carry anything or anyone that might be a load, so that you can ease on down the road. Take one step at a time, and ease on down the road. You see, sometimes this road may be lonely, sometimes you will take one step forward and then two steps backwards. Those backward steps are just mistakes; brush yourself off and ease on down the road. As you go down this road, you might find a group of people that are trying to move down the road like you are, and well, that's great. It may be an organization, or a person. For me, it was my sister, and we are easing down the road together, along with a wonderful group of other new upcoming authors.

In the Wiz, Dorothy is fortunate to meet a group who is trying to move down the road too. Her group includes the scarecrow, who needed a brain, and later, there was the tin man who wanted a heart and finally the lion who wanted courage. Let's take a little from all of them. Of course, we'll start with my favorite, the scarecrow. I know we have talked about him a little. He just wanted a brain. The most amazing thing about this, is that he was the smartest. He was the one that was always coming up with solutions. He was the one that was always quoting something. Then there was the tin man who said he needed a heart, or so he thought. But he loved and cared more than them all. He would put others before himself. And finally, there was the lion. The crying scary lion. Who has ever seen such a thing? He roared like a kitten because he had forgotten who he was and was seeking courage.

What can you learn from all of them? Let's see. For one, if you listen to the witch and the crows in your life, you will forget what you are made of. You will forget that God has already equipped you with everything that you need to succeed! If you listen to other negative individuals for an extended period, you will start to internalize all that negativity and eventually, it can stop you from moving forward, simply because you don't think that you are smart enough. You can't allow people to turn you away from what is near and dear to your heart. If you choose to turn away from your dreams, you give in to despair and become increasingly miserable. You can become so miserable that you feel nothing, and begin to shuffle through life because you can no longer feel your heartbeat.

When you make mistakes, don't cry about it and make yourself rusty to the point that you can't move. Just have someone there to hold you accountable. Have someone there that will slide a little oil to you. When you get stuck you will need someone to help you get unstuck.

That's why I'm here. That is why I'm am writing this book for you. It's my way of sliding a little oil to you. Sometimes you may need some oil in your arms, some in your legs, elbows, etc.; wherever you're dried up, you will need to get oiled. Some areas you can reach and some you can't. I got you. I will just slide some oil in you. It may not be STD Oil but I assure you, Crisco will do just fine. Do this and I promise you, you will not become like the lion who roars (actually meows) like a kitten! You will not listen to the witch and consequently forget that you are the king of your jungle.

I did not say you would not get afraid at some point. When growing your business, you will be afraid of the dark, afraid of running into lions, tigers and bears (OH MY!). Fear of running a business is real. You're thinking, *Can I really do this? Do I have enough money? Will anyone use my services, and if they do will they be pleased?* Don't allow the fear to stop you. Go see the wizard. Yes me, I am your wizard, and I am real and available. The scarecrow was not afraid of the witch; he was only afraid of fire because he was made of straw. However, he was not so afraid that he did not go to see the wizard to get want he wanted. Did you get that? The tin man was not afraid of fire or the witch. He was only afraid of the rain because he would rust. Again, he was not so afraid that he did go after what he wanted. Finally, there is the lion who was afraid of everything, even his own shadow. But not even the lion let fear stop him from going after what he really wanted.

At some point, they all came face to face with the witch and the witch's advantage was that she knew each of their fears. Interestingly, when she threw the scarecrow a ball of fire, the tin man put it out. She made it rain, so the tin man would rust, but the others just slid some oil to him! The poor lion just fainted at the mere sight of her presence, but the others were there to revive him. Don't give your witch the power. You have the power to win! You have not allowed all those witches, lions, tigers and bears to stop you thus far; and I don't want you to look back now. I want you to ease on down that road. I want you to follow the yellow brick road and know that you can. Surround yourself with people that will help you get to a brand-new day. Stand tall and strong and know that you are great. Know that you are a lion in your own way. I want you to continue to have courage. I want you to know that every day is a brand-new day.

The bottom linc is that you must believe. Your mind is very powerful. What you think about becomes what you believe, and that is what you will achieve. You have got to believe it in your heart. Believe what you feel. You must believe that you can do whatever is necessary to achieve your goals to help your Baby grow. What you say, what you think, what you watch, will all influence what you do and what you believe. And finally, if you believe in your Baby, no one can change your thoughts! You have got to believe that you can and will grow this business. It is not necessary to click your heels 3 times, but if that's what you need to do to believe, then do that. But you have got to believe to achieve. You must believe in yourself right from the start. You've got to believe in the magic in your heart. I am telling you this because it's true. You've got to believe in yourself, yes, as much as I believe in you. You have to feel it. You have to feel good.

At my previous church, they had us say the same scripture for more than 20 years at the beginning of each service. They don't say 'good morning, will you please stand?' They don't start any music, and they don't ask you to bow your head. They simply say, "This the day the Lord has made, we will rejoice and be glad in it" (Psalm 118:24). No matter what you are doing, who you are talking to, what you are reading; you would stop and stand up and clap, and then the music begins. They have told us that the Lord has made this day, and we have been blessed to see it and that we Will Rejoice and be Glad. They did not ask us if we would rejoice and be glad they told us that we would. And guess what? We do just that. So, speak it. Say it. Talk to yourself, and talk about what is going to be. Speak about your success. Speak it. Let's not talk about what's wrong, that doesn't fix anything. Let's only talk about the solution. This works for everything in life. If there is a problem, then there's is a solution. We have just got to keep still, and give that one thing our attention. Yes, be still, and be quiet; so, you can hear and receive the solution. The same goes for what you think.

The mind is so powerful that you do what your mind tells you to do. So, as a man thinketh in his heart, so is he. (Proverbs 23:7) You've got to watch what you put in your mind! Pay attention to what you are focusing on, and it will become bigger. Oh, you don't believe me? Is there a part of your body you don't seem to like? If there is, every time you look in the mirror that is what you will see. That one grey hair, that one bump. Your arms, butt, stomach, whatever you focus on; that's what you see. That is why it is important to have goals, so you will know where your business is going. You have to see it, and you have to see it in a positive way. Don't see yourself as stressed, see yourself with order and success. Don't see yourself with just a little, but see yourself with an abundance. See yourself at your best. Don't worry about what others will think or say. That is absolutely none of your business. Your business is about you handling your business. Growing your Baby. See it and do the work to make it happen.

Let's touch a minute on goal setting and prioritizing. I know that I have talked to you about knowing what your tomorrow will look like, but I will go into this a little more in the next chapter. For now, I want you to know this: when you set your goal, do the most important things first. It is possible for you to keep busy all day, and yet get nothing accomplished. This happens because none of what you did that day was important and you need to do the important things first. I learned at an early age to do what's most important first, but I will credit Stephen Covey since he did such an awesome job stressing this in his book *The 7 Habits of Highly Effective People*.

Covey shared that to be effective, you have to do the most important thing first. He even takes it a step further, stressing that it has everything to do with your being productive. Once you do what is important and Urgent; then, you can excel. You often want to put this task off because it's something that you don't want to do or some news you don't want to deliver, or some bad piece of information.

We had to lay off some employees once at my brother's company in Louisiana. We were laying off all the part-time help. Now I advised the manager to do it when she first got there because she had such a close relationship with the staff and I didn't want her to stress herself out any more, than was necessary. She already had to wait until that afternoon because they were all part time and only worked evenings. She dreaded it, as she should have. You should never become comfortable with firing anyone. It should never feel good, even if it's their own fault. Well, she finally did it as soon as they were all there, and they ended up consoling her. Some of them were tired of working two jobs anyway. Others said they knew that she depended on them, but that they would be ok. It was over and she eventually felt better. There is beauty, after all, in doing what you have to do!

You Are A Wiz At This Pregnancy Thing Takeaways:

- You must believe
- Beware of your witches, lions, tigers and bears
- Have a crew, person or organization that can slide some oil to you when you need. Visit www.bookdebbieporter.com
- Do the most important thing first
- See it and believe it; so that you can achieve it

THIRD
TRIMESTER

CHAPTER 7

TICK TOCK: IT'S TIME TO GET UNCOMFORTABLE

Hello, it's a new phase! Now you are in the third trimester, and all you want to do, all the time, is head to your home stretch. You are beginning to see major changes. The extra weight that you've gained is beginning to put added pressure on your back, making it feel uncomfortable.

Ok, let me translate for you again. Your business is growing by leaps and bounds. You are seeing major changes in the growth of your Baby. The work load and new clients are putting so much added pressure on you. You are loving the change, and are excited, yet uncomfortable. Here is where you have really got to start tightening the rope.

This is the stage where you must use all of your time wisely. Your time is the most valuable thing that you have, even if you don't know it yet. You must learn how to find more time within the same 24 hours. You can do it. One thing about time, is that it is an even playing field. No one has more time than someone else. Everyone has the same 24 hours. Oprah Winfrey, Steve Harvey, the President of the United States of America, teachers, college professors, professional athletes, students, our parents, our managers, our pool cleaners, nursery school workers, preachers, doctors, grocery store owners, our hairstylists, and lawyers. Everyone has the same 24 hours. The thing is, no one can re-negotiate with God for more time. It is an even playing field. I only have one suggestion regarding this: USE YOUR 24 HOURS WISELY. I recommend that you make every minute count. Remember, I already said you should know what your tomorrow looks like, and this is why…so that you can use your 24 hours wisely. For you to control and get the most out of your 24 hours, you need to know where you are headed.

You do not have the luxury of time to just wake up in the morning, lay there and say, "I wonder what I have to do today". Do you think that any successful person is able to do that while they are in the building stage? Absolutely not. I recently heard Oprah on the radio promoting her new show Greenleaf, which I love by the way; and she said she was working as if the rent was due. We all know that Oprah, the billionaire has enough money to pay the rent. What she was implying was how busy she was, and how hard she's been working to make sure her station succeeds. After all, she was on the Tom Joyner morning show, promoting her show. We can never get too big or too busy to sell our business. That's right! We should never get too comfortable to sell or promote our business. When we become too busy for our business, then we are probably too big for our own good, and need to take a step back so that we can show up. The president of the United States has help, and a lot of it, but he still has to show up. Oprah has help, and a lot of it, here again she shows up. Although the professional athlete has made it, he still goes to practice, and tries to further his career, that is, they always show up. They all show up to be successful in their various fields.

You must manage your time, if not, it will get away from you. I am a person that is very time conscious. I don't like wasting my time or anyone else's. I remember when my children were born, I had to learn to give myself extra time to do everything. I had been married for about 5 years before my first baby was born. Since they are only two years apart, we went from 0 to 100. I would prep as much as I could, the night before. I would make sure I had everything laid out, everything that I could put in the car the night before, I did. I would prepare to leave 10 minutes earlier and it never failed that one of them would mess up their clothes or I would forget something that I had to have. It didn't take me long to figure out that I needed an extra 30 minutes, just to take the rush out of my morning. I hate rushing. I don't rush, I plan. Time is something that can quickly get away from you, especially if you don't have plans for it. It is like money. You know how it is when you break a $20 bill; once you break it, it leaves you and you don't know where it went, and what you spent it on. Time is the same way.

Once you think you have extra time and start to do nothing, or what I call fiddling, you will lose track of it. Let's talk about fiddling for a minute. I fiddle now, because the menopause thing is messing with me. Me; a fiddler (never). I mean I have to put in an extra 10 minutes into my schedule for fiddling. Sorry, it still bothers me, so I just had to release that. Anyway, we were comparing money to time and talking about how fast it can get away from us. Time is like now you have it, and before you know it, you don't have it. It's here and then it's gone. We must be aware of our time stealers and prepare to leave extra time for them.

Our next time robber is a big one. It's called ***procrastination.*** We all procrastinate sometimes, yes all of us do. See if you are familiar with any of these statements:

- Wait, I'll do it later
- I will do it in a minute

- I will do it tomorrow
- I'm "gonna" do it

All of these statements equal procrastination. This is something that can really cost us time. We've all done it. Do you snooze when your alarm clock goes off? Yes, that's another form of procrastination. When I was in college, I was the worst procrastinator of all. I would snooze two or three times, simply because I did not want to get up. I probably had done something constructive with my time after going to class and work, such as going to a party the night before. I would snooze, snooze and then snooze some more. I just hated being awakened by an alarm clock. It felt like if the alarm clock woke me up, I did not get enough sleep. I usually sleep for seven to eight hours, so I figured out what time I needed to go to bed to ensure that I get at least seven hours of sleep and wake up without the aid of an alarm clock. I am not suggesting that you try not snoozing, this is just very practical advice about what I do that works. During the last 30 minutes of my sleep, I am just gathering my thoughts. So, snoozing, I am all too familiar with. My advice here, is to get enough sleep. When you are rested, you perform better. Your mind is sharper.

Procrastination is something that you need to be very much aware of, and just be aware that you are doing it. One way to help with procrastination, that we discussed earlier, is to do what you don't want to do and get it out of the way. We talked about doing the most important things first. However, the most important thing may not even be the thing that you are dreading. It may not even be the thing that has you stuck. I still recommend that you get the most important thing done first, then do the thing that has you stuck, next. Sometimes, we just can't move to do what needs to be done because of this one thing that we don't want to do or face. Do it, so you can move on. Do it so that you can get unstuck. Do it, so it will not have power over you. Like Nike says, just do it!

Think about how people have put their dreams on hold because they have procrastinated. I often wonder what my life would look like right now if I had just sat down and written this book 20 years ago. Well the truth is, it would not have been this particular book, but I have always had a book in me. What I did not have, was the discipline to sit down to write it. I was always going to do it. I was going to, once I got my business started. I was going to, once I finally hired someone to handle the meetings for me. I was always "going to." Then I had two babies, that's all I need to say. Two babies and two businesses, equals no book, and it's such a great excuse. Well, I am glad the procrastination about that is over and I am glad that I am helping you avoid some of the same mistakes that I have made.

I don't know if you had been putting off starting your business, or if you've been putting off growing your already existing business; but I'm glad that you are on track now. Stay focused. Don't put off tomorrow, what you can do today. Don't act like me and say I will do it tomorrow morning and make your morning crazier than it already is. Be better than me. Have you ever been so sleepy or lazy, you couldn't get out of the bed? You couldn't even do everything you needed to prepare for the next day? So, you decide to keep your lazy self in bed and just think about what you are going to wear. Oh, I'm the only one? Really? Ok, thanks for your honesty, but I will use me as an example. I will lay in bed and figure out my outfit, jewelry, shoes, purse, how I'm putting my make up on, and what I am going to grab quickly for breakfast. Ok I'm good. I get up to get dressed the next morning, all is going well especially since I hit the snoozer only three times before I eventually get up. I am completely dressed, and all I have to do is put my shoes on, and I cannot find one of them, dang it! There it is, great, I found the shoe, I run to grab something to eat, put everything in the car, attempt to start the car and there are no keys. I did not think about keys because I always keep my keys in the same spot, and if they are not there, I don't know where to look. Time is gone. Man, if I had just snoozed two times instead of three, I would be ok. I don't know where my keys are. Ok what did I wear yesterday? Nope; not there. What did I do when I got home? Think Porter think. Let's see, I pulled up in the garage and I had to go to the bathroom. I ran into the house, turned the security alarm off, used the bathroom and went into the kitchen to speak to hubby. Ok, I will go and look in the kitchen. No keys, dang it! Where are they? Let me check the bathroom, right quick. I know they are not there because… Yep, there they are, right there on the sink, in the bathroom, where I left them! Now I'm late, shoot, I should have only snoozed once.

Are you getting this, the stress, the pressure, the rushing? It is not worth it. Get up. Get everything ready, and Get out. You know I told you that my husband was very routine, right? He comes home from work every day. He goes upstairs, empties his gym bag, and re-packs it for the next day. He then sits his clothes out for the next day. And he does all this before he even eats dinner! Every single day for 28 years. I think it is absolutely sickening, especially since I am incapable of doing this **every single day**. Oh, and by the way he never, ever, snoozes!

The more your Baby grows, the more you need to be in control of your time. You need to know your schedule, your children's schedule and your husband's schedule. Why is this so important? It is important so that you can AVOID being stressed. What good does it do to have a perfect schedule planned if you have to attend a football game that you didn't have on your planner? Your schedule is not going to work; if you fail to add other important events from your children's or husband's schedule. This becomes even more difficult as your children become older. When they are young, all invites come to you, but as they get older, they are in more control of their schedule and they share it with you on an 'as needed basis; which is usually at the last minute.

Multiple schedules and multiple roles will require you to apply your energy management. Energy Management is defined as the process of monitoring, controlling and conserving energy. Don't use up your energy planning, without taking all things into consideration. Let's not compare our 24 hours to that of a coworker or friend. I want to help you determine how you work best. Are you running a marathon or a sprint? Some of you run marathons, and marathons require a steady pace. If that works for you, to get the best out of your day, go with that. For others, like myself (I actually get more energy from the sprint,) and I use the downtime to prepare for the next sprint. My husband runs a marathon and I sprint. One is no better than the other. It's like the doer and the delegator; you just need to determine what gives you the most energy.

You will also need physical and mental breaks throughout the day, especially since you work from home. It might be a walk around the block or just going to run a few errands. Just a short break can help you gain more energy and be more productive. Deloitte Consulting LLP's National Managing Director Amy Feirn, talks about becoming a professional pretzel, which simply means, twisting into someone other than yourself. Feirn states "Trying to be someone you're not is hard work. It drains your energy!" When we stop fighting against our strengths and start using them, we unleash energy rather than consume it.

Don't forget that I am here to help you work out those details; so that you can have every opportunity to give your business, yourself, your family and friends the attention that they desire. Visit www.bookdebbieporter.com, if you desire additional coaching.

You know the saying that if you want something done, give it to a busy person. Does that even make sense? Why would you even consider giving it to a busy person? Because busy people get things done. If they are doers be careful, just make sure they don't already have too much on their plate. However, remember; a doer likes to do and if they tell you that they are going to do something, you can usually depend on them to do it. The delegator is just as busy, trying to make sure that everything she has given out to everyone is accomplished and checking on them all to see how she can help. The delegator is usually a person that does not mind saying no, especially if she knows she has no one else to delegate it to. But if by chance she accepts it, you can consider it done because she does not trust herself to remember to do it, so she will do it quickly because she wants it off her plate. If possible, she will do it, or get it done right then. The saying is true, if you want it done, give it to a busy person. I think you have this part down. My reminders to you are: try not to procrastinate, and if you must, keep it to a minimum.

Remember, do what is important first, prepare, take all schedules into consideration, and give it to a busy person. This will help take some of the pressure off of you so you won't be so uncomfortable. Tick Tock; your 24 hours are running out.

TAKEAWAYS for Tick-Tock: It's Time to Get Uncomfortable:

- Everyone has the same 24 hours each day, use yours wisely
- Promote your business like your rent is due, tomorrow
- To avoid the need to rush, prepare the night before
- Make sure you have your schedule and your family's schedule, so that you can make realistic plans
- Determine your energy management. Do you run marathons or sprints?

CHAPTER 8
THE WOBBLING WALK: THE POWER OF SUPPORT

During pregnancy, growth happens in phases. At this stage of your pregnancy, your baby should truly be growing. You might even begin to feel mild contractions, which are preparing you for labor. It's called Braxton Hicks contractions, false contractions which are simply preparing you for the real labor.

Translation: Your business, your Baby is full term. You have taken most of the necessary steps to ensure that you will birth a healthy Baby when the time for delivery comes. You are almost there, but again, let us consider a few more things which we must put in place. After all, we don't want to have come this far, only to discover that we still have some major problems!

You need support, and good relationships, so that this Baby will be set for life. You want to make sure that you surround yourself with the things and people you will need. You have done an outstanding job thus far. I just want to make sure that you are maintaining those good relationships as you go on. You want to make sure that you are holding on tightly to those good relationships, both personal ones, and in business. Make sure you have a solid foundation with family, real friends, children, your banker, suppliers, your mechanic, your printer, etc. Make certain that you let them know that they are appreciated and that ultimately, your relationship with them isn't one sided. Show and tell them that they can depend on you the same way you have depended and leaned on them this last year.

Be in the moment, wherever you are. When I am speaking, or doing a presentation, I always tell this story about how people see me. The people at my children's school didn't think that I worked, while the people that I did business with probably thought that I was a bad mother or wife; or that I tell my husband what to do. To think any of those things, just means that you really don't know me. The truth is, I try my very best to be in the moment wherever I am. When I was at the school chaperoning my child's trip or selling tickets for an event, I was all in. I have had my current home-based business for 17 years; and people at my daughter's school did not know it until her junior year in high school. Oh well, I was not there to sell my business or to talk about it! I was there to be Mom.

Let's now talk a little about developing great business relationships. I will use my business as an example. I make sure that I have great relationships with my vendors, my bank, my mechanic, printer, employees, etc. For example, I went on vacation and there were problems with my van; the drivers knew that they could take the van to my mechanic, he repaired it and the mechanic knew that I would pay him when I returned. You want to know the name of the people at your bank and more importantly, you want them to know your name and love to see you walk through the door. You want to be different from others. You should take the time to get to know them so that you can have a real conversation with them. The truth? They can bend some rules for you; believe me. While I am talking about banking, make sure you have some money for a stormy day. We try to live a debt free life; however, I do have a line of credit and savings for a

STORMY day. This savings is NOT for a rainy day. Don't just go into your savings for any and everything. Wait for the STORM.

You want your employees to appreciate your leadership and you want to let them know that you value what they do. With that knowledge in mind, they will go the extra mile for you. I am requiring you to read Kenneth Blanchard's The One Minute Manager and Gung Ho. There are some horrible managers out here, but please don't be one of them. I don't care where I go to receive service; if there is a problem, it is the management's fault. Take responsibility for everything because it's your fault. You must lead. People expect to be led. Let me drop a footnote here. Early in the book I talked about doers and delegator, I also shared that I would be the worst clerk that you would ever have. If you are not a manager, hire you a good one and then LET THEM MANAGE. Nothing can ruin a business and stunt a business's growth more than not having a great manager. Owning a business, and telling people what to do does not make you a manager.

I must commend my brother Kelvin here. He has a business and he is a marketing genius, however; he understood that he needed a manager. He hired an awesome District Manager, Kim, to manage his company and Kim has hired several managers to help her. My dad calls her the sixth child in our family and I call her Kimmie. We have been connected on so many different levels and stages of life that I would not know where to start. She is now my boss and book editor. Go on amazon and purchase her book, "The Assignment: Discovering & Living in Your Purpose." Now we can get back to the lesson, but I had to get that in, also.

So, stay in your lane. Do what you do best. Listen to your employees and remember that they are people with real feelings. Let your requirements be known, and motivate them to a point that they will want to make you look good. Even then, be a leader. Read the book Gung Ho. It is a very short and quick book.

Make sure that you are available for family and real friends. When I owned an event planning company, I would have to lean on my family and friends to help me. Sometimes I would have five events in one weekend. However, I could not be everywhere at once. What helped me is that I knew that I had awesome employees, family, and friends that would take care of the business, just as I would. They had my best interest at heart. Don't forget where you have come from and who helped you to get there. If my family and friends were not available to work, I did not make them feel bad. It's life, and they have one to live also. If by chance they were not available, I understood, and I didn't have any hard feelings. Remember that word NO? If they were not available, I loved the fact that they just said it, because it allowed me to make other plans. I loved that they respected their time and mine. My childhood friend Carol, who is really a big sister has a business near my house. She knows that she can call me anytime for the smallest things, like "Can you go and turn my AC on for me?" I don't mind at all. If I can I go or if I can't, we are still friends, and it won't stop her from asking me the next time.

Years ago, my family used to host a celebrity basketball game where celebrities would donate their time to play basketball for more than 5,000 spectators. This annual game was one of our major fundraisers for our nonprofit organization. Since my brother Rodney played in the NFL, it was easy to get NFL players, along with some NBA players. In addition to them we would have some of the actors and actresses that were on some of the most popular TV shows at the time. Some played in movies, while others were top music makers in their field. Looking back, it was truly an impressive event!

We had one celebrity that used to come to my mom's house, every year before we started having this event. He, along with his siblings, would just come into town and hang out at my mom's---to eat dinner, laugh, talk and play games. He had been in a few things, but would not have been considered a huge celebrity, at that time. He was chasing his dream, but just had not hit it big yet. For the first celebrity game, he came and was just glad to be a part of it. About three years later, he had gotten a leading role in a movie and was too busy to come to the game. No problem. We understood, we loved him and wished him well. The final year, he decided to come because other celebrities that had attended were giving the event such rave reviews, and commended the events growth. I was always in charge of talent acquisition and airline travel arrangements. When I called this person, he would not accept my call. I was told I now had to call his agent, to book him. *Well, ok then.* I contacted his agent. Let me just say out of all the people that were there, we paid no one and spoke to no one's agent. Most of the celebrity participants were celebrity friends of celebrity friends and had heard about this wonderful event and wanted to be involved. But the person we were close to, the person that used to come to my mom's house just to hang out wanted us to go through his agent. If you noticed I have not mentioned any names, because I'm way too lazy and busy to take the time to call and get approval. But the absence of celebrity names doesn't change this story.

Anyway, I called his agent, and she wanted to know what her client would be doing from the time he got here. No problem, I told her that I would fax her an itinerary for the entire weekend. Yes faxed; there were no emails then. His agent called back and said, "Mrs. Porter, I received the itinerary and I need some more details." I said, "This is the same one that we have sent to all of the other celebrities." She said "Yes, but I'm going to need a little more information. "I said "Okay, no problem." I went and tweaked the itinerary to meet what I thought were her requirements and faxed it again. She called again. I was expecting to hear her praises because I had typed it myself and I've already told you I'm not clerical. When I answered the call, she said, "I received your itinerary and it is still not detailed enough." I replied, "Ok, I need for you to help me out; I don't know how I can get any more detailed without giving you what they are doing minute by minute." Her reply was, "That is exactly what I want. I need to know from the time he wakes up, what he will be doing. Where will he be eating and what time he will leave the restaurant. If the car is going back to the hotel, what time should it arrive, etc." I said, "Ms., I know your client very well. Tell him that Debbie said, I love him, but I am not working that hard. I have given you a detailed itinerary and he can attend or not. Please let me know his decision, so I will know whether or not to give his airline tickets to someone else." Of course, she called back about five minutes later and said that her client would be attending our event. When he arrived, he had truly become a celebrity in every sense of the word. He had forgotten the people that were there for him in the beginning. This person worked us harder than any other celebrity that weekend.

See we didn't understand special treatment for celebrities. We had a celebrity in our family. I guess, that's how other people see my brother Rodney. He was never a celebrity at home, he was just a son, dad, friend, uncle, brother, and a baby brother at that. I think that's why he loved being home because he could just be himself and no one would treat him any differently. He still had to take out the trash, run to the store to get mom an onion while she was cooking, make up his bed, play monopoly and get fussed at for smoking up the house while he was cooking a hamburger. Subsequently, we did not know how to treat a celebrity that we considered a friend any differently. We were just trying to do what we had always done, which was treat people the way we wanted to be treated. But, oh well. Be teachable. Never get too big to learn. You can always learn something. Keep good relationships, you never know who you are going to need!

TAKEAWAYS for The Wobbling Act: The Power of Support

- Maintain good relationships with everyone in your business and personal life
- Be in the moment, wherever you are
- Read Gung Ho by Ken Blanchard
- Be teachable, no matter how big your Baby gets

CHAPTER 9
LABOR: THE BALANCING ACT

Yes! We made it to the final event. Now that you are in labor, you must learn to balance it all, because, finally, the Baby is coming! Balance is important to both you and your Baby. As hard as it might be, you must take the time to relax and breathe because it will make your Labor a little easier. It is of the utmost importance. The Baby is in position for arrival and you must prioritize what is important in your life. Outside of what is important to you, I would like to talk about some areas that are completely non-negotiable. Areas like: narrow business service, clutter, vacation, and finally, you.

Have you ever tried to give something that you did not have? I have. I remember being burnt out. I was building a business, trying to purchase a home, I presided over the youth department at my church, and in addition to that, I had lived through three or four miscarriages at the time. I had an empty cup; yet I was still trying to pour into others. God sat me down, and I was so glad he did and that I was even more glad that I listened.

You must take time to just chill. Be still even if it's only for a couple of hours, a day, a long weekend, a week or a couple of weeks. At some point, you must regroup. When it comes to your business, you must decide on what you will and will not do. What services will you perform? You must decide and stand firm on it or you will be all over the place.

I have shared with you that I had an event planning service. I planned class reunions. That's all I did. During that time, I would get requests to plan weddings, family reunions, corporate events and any other event that you could think of that was not a class reunion. I would turn those requests away because that was not what I did. That was not what I specialized in. I planned class reunions, period. That's what I was set up to do. I knew every detail about a class reunion from A-Z, and I was good at it. People would often say, you should do weddings, or family reunions. I would say "That's not what we do. We plan class reunions. There are companies that might dabble in it all but we plan class reunions, only. If you want a great class reunion, I am your girl." Now could I have done weddings? Yes. Could I have done family reunions and corporate events? Yes. However, that WAS NOT WHAT I DID! I only did class reunions, and there were more than enough of them to keep me busy. I would do about 40-50 reunions per summer, and I was the number one reunion planning company in the city. Why? I focused my company's business narrowly and provided the best service for the best price.

The next area that you must master is clutter. Clutter often tells you what's going on in your life. Clutter can affect your mind, your ability to focus and process; it can also cause depression and unnecessary stress. Now I am not a doctor or a specialist in this area, I am just speaking from practical experience on how it makes me feel. When I have clutter around me, it stops me from meeting my goals and my mind is really all over the place. Clutter can clutter your mind. Have you ever walked into a bank and seen clutter, even a cluttered desk? The answer is probably no. Imagine if you did. Go ahead—imagine it. How much confidence would you place in that bank or representative? I always say that if my desk and my car is a mess, so is my mind. When I can get my house cleaned, wash my hair, clean my desk and my car; it simply communicates to me that the world is as it should be.

Let me google this quickly to see what google has to say about it. Ok, here is an article in Life Optimized, about "The effects of Clutter in your Business and Life" let me see what it says. Hey, I was right on track. This is how this article opens in bold letters. "I don't know about you, but clutter distracts one from being able to fully focus on what's important." WOW!! You would have thought that I had gone to this article first when I was only just sharing how clutter affected me. I will give you two things from here because I don't want to start pulling from the article at this point; nor do I want to spend too much time on this area.

The two things that they talk about here are how clutter affects you and your business. One, when your environment or mind is cluttered and feels chaotic, you can't focus fully, and it goes on to talk about how it can affect you mentally, emotionally and create stress. Secondly, it talks about how clutter makes it more difficult to find things when you need them which can be stressful! Even digital information, like passwords. (This is something I need to work on). However, they do share 3 key things we need in place to de-clutter our environment.

1. Systems (to know where things go)
2. Decisiveness (to avoid having things pile up)
3. Maintenance (so things stay de-cluttered)

Enough about clutter, this next area is one of my favorites. Vacation.

When you have a home-based business, vacations are a must. You work from home. You must get away. Even if it is just for the weekend. Even though I suggest longer. You need to be able to sleep in someone else's bed and allow them to make it up; have someone cook breakfast without having to do the dishes; lay out by the pool, and think about nothing while also doing nothing. When you allow yourself to do and think about nothing you will come back ready for the world. Now I know it takes quite a bit of work to prepare to get away, but believe me it is worth it. I go on vacation every year and staycations as well, in between. Sometimes we take the children and at least once a year, for our anniversary weekend, it's just me and my hubby. We look for any excuse to get away for a moment. When I go on vacation, it feels like I have fallen off the face of the earth. I don't want you to call me for any reason, concerning business. I will leave a list of business contacts, friends and family members employees should call if there is an emergency. If you call me, that means that it is so serious that I need to come home and I never, ever want to receive that call. But a call because the van is broken or someone broke into the van or other customer issues? No! I am on vacation. Besides, this goes back to relationships. If the van breaks down, take it to my mechanic, he will fix it and I will pay him when I get back. If it won't start, call AAA. If someone breaks in the van, bursts a window or something, we have insurance. And if your employees don't know what to do, you have left emergency numbers of people that can make those decisions. Consequently, all above examples have happened while I was on vacation, and none of this resulted in a call to me. My employees, mechanic and family handled it. I was on vacation. Run away, everything will be ok.

Then, there is YOU. You are the most important thing on this list, remember there is no replacement for you. Here are some small suggestions that have worked for me. At this stage in your business take Fridays off. I would always take Fridays, along with Saturday and Sundays off. If Fridays don't work for you, pick a day. However, make it your day. Friday was the day that I went to the beauty shop, got my nails/feet done, went to lunch with a friend or by myself, got a massage and relaxed. Whatever I needed or wanted to do, I did it on Fridays. When my daughter was a baby, my mother-in-law would keep her every Friday. Well, I had her first two grandchildren so I was afforded a little extra treatment. Fridays was her time with her grandchildren and a day for me. My husband was also scheduled to pick them up from her on Fridays. On Fridays, I did not talk work. That was my fun day. That was my day not to worry about work or anything else. Just me. It made me a better boss, wife, mother and friend.

Other little secrets are tiny things like, plan/prepare meals for the week. Have a schedule and stick to it. Make sure that your children are on a schedule, and stick to it. Children resist routine but they love it. That's why the school system does the same thing at school, at the same time every week.

Finally, when you spend time with your children and your spouse, unless there is something major going on and you absolutely have to be distracted, let it be their time! Always, always, always, make it clear that they come first.

TAKEAWAYS for Labor-The Balancing Act:

- Decide what is a priority in your life
- Have a narrow business focus so you can be the expert
- Declutter your life
- Take vacations, and staycations
- Make sure your spouse/children know and feel that they come first

CONCLUSION-DELIVERY

Congratulations on your full term, healthy Baby. I knew you could do it, and I am so glad that you allowed me to coach you through this process! I know that you could have done it without me, however, I am so glad that you hired me to make it easier for you. Thank you for allowing me to share this book with you, and for investing in yourself. I want you to know that I understand that this may have been a challenging task and I am glad you decided to invest in yourself and fight for what you really wanted.

I have one final confession to make, that my writing coach does not even know about. Although, I have always wanted to write a book, I have fought this process all the way. I fought against myself. I hired a coach, which is what I would suggest to anyone who is trying to achieve any goal. I will be the first to admit that there is no way that I would have sat still long enough to write this book; if I had not invested time and money with a coach. Not only that, I would have made many unnecessary mistakes. When I say that I have fought this from day one, I mean just that. You see; originally my sister and I had hired the same coach except she was writing her own book and I was going to use a ghostwriter, before I found and hired this coach. Two different programs, both wonderful, but just different. Something just called to me about the program and so, I just decided to give it a try and hire the coach. The next day, I started second guessing myself and decided that I was not going to do this program. (Fear) remember, lions and tiger and bears. I had three days to cancel; which by the way, I had every intention of doing; you recall us talking about procrastination. That's exactly what happened. My intentions were to cancel the next day, and I got busy and missed my deadline-- the first sign that I was not supposed to cancel.

Then I decided, me being so smart, that I will just sell it to someone that I mentor. We went to lunch that Friday and she was open to buying it. My husband and I were teaching a class at church the same week and I had already studied and prepared for the class. I came home with a solution to sell this program and just hire a ghostwriter writer. I sat down to look over my lesson for class and being the over-achiever that I am, I decided to answer a few questions in the writing workbook. Within 30 minutes I had the answer that I did not want. I HAD TO WRITE MY OWN BOOK.

Now I already knew that writing this book is what I had been told to do. In part because I have other books inside of me and I needed to know how to write a book so that I can write others. I was just out of my comfort zone. You think that I would have stopped there, but my strong will wouldn't let me. I finally accepted the fact that I was writing this book, after I had already wasted two weeks. I then began to pray to enjoy the program, since I had been fighting it, and I did just that. But something was still missing. I prayed and asked for direction. I did not know what it was, I was not enjoying writing my book. God answered again. Every week I had to turn in an assignment before I could even begin to write my book. I had gotten every assignment approved. Excited as I was, something was still missing. As I was headed into week four of the class, I submitted my assignment on Outcomes. This assignment explained what I wanted my ideal reader to get out of this book. My original book was about, living a balanced life. This is what my coach sent back to me once I turned in that assignment:

> *I can approve this. I will say "Balance" is very difficult to get people to invest in and I think you will have trouble selling this. You did follow the instructions and it's passable. I think there are easier books you can write about balance that'll solve a specific problem, and people are already investing in solving. But you can consider this approved unless you want to dig deeper.*

Fifteen minutes later, I received a second message from her: She obviously went back and read my assignment that identified my ideal reader. This was her reply:

> *Based on your ideal reader, your outcome should be a program to "help her start a new home-based business" and balance gets tucked in there but it isn't a generic program on balance. That's my recommendation anyway.*

My reply: I am willing to dig deeper. I would love, love, love to write a book on starting your home-based business.

That's it! Now today, I have my answer and I am excited. I am excited and scared. It is spring break and my birthday week and I am already behind three weeks. I must redo the lessons that I had previously completed, because my book just changed, and I am super excited. Did I share with you that my book must be completely done by April 25th and I just received this text on March 10th. What do I do? What would I tell my ideal reader to do? I would tell her to take off, have fun, laugh, and enjoy herself, her family and her friends. Yes, I did just that. Both of my daughters were home from college, for spring break and I took time off to hang out with my girls for a week. I had a blast, and then I went in to crazy nerd mode. Today is Sunday, the 9th of April 2017. I just came home from church and I have finished my book. My Book wasn't due until April 25th, but I gave myself a deadline of April 15th (Tax Day). Guess what? I finished on the 9th of April.

Thank God, I finally listened and did not try to do this myself. I have learned two major lessons:

1. Hire a coach to make life easier. Go to www.bookdebbieporter.com
2. I can really do all things through Christ who strengthens me!

SUGGESTED READINGS

The Assignment: Discovering & Living in Your Purpose by Kim Porter

Bring Out the Millionaire in You by Angela Dees

Gung Ho by Ken Blanchard

Jump by Steve Harvey

The One Minute Manger by Kenneth Blanchard

The Power of a Praying Women by Stormie Omartian

Your Best Life Now by Joel Osteen

Who Moved My Cheese? By Spencer Johnson

ACKNOWLEDGEMENTS

Reginald, my loving husband of 28 years, thank you for always supporting and encouraging me to be a better me. Thank you for reminding me for the last 20 years that I was supposed to write a book. In addition, I want to say how much I love you for eating whatever you could find while I was writing. Did I hear you say that's nothing new? LOL!!! Love you and thanks.

Dana and Devin my babies, yes, even though you are grown you will always be my babies. I love you and thanks to both of you for your patience, your support and your help.

To my mom and dad thank you for always encouraging me and raising me to honor God. Thank you for always believing in me and setting the bar high.

Angela, my sister, the peanut butter to my jelly. Thanks for it all. I have enjoyed the journey so far. Thank you for encouraging me to write my own book and not hire a ghostwriter. Even when I did not feel capable of doing so. Thanks for pushing me off the cliff—my parachute did open.

To my siblings including in-laws, uncle, aunts, cousins, friends and all of my awesome nieces and nephews, thank you all for always supporting me and being happy for me. Thanks also for helping me get Amazon #1 Bestseller status.

Amanda, thank you for my company name, The Business Renovator and for always designing whatever I needed; even in the middle of the night while your babies were asleep. You will receive one babysitting coupon. No, not two just one.

Sherry, how do I begin to say thank you for allowing me to read each chapter to you as I finished. Now after 20+ years, you and my hubby can finally stop asking me when am I going to write my book. They call us Lucy and Ethel for good reason. Of course, you are Lucy although I know you will disagree. Lol!

To my early readers, and proofreaders, Andetria, Angie, Carol, Charmaine, Cheryl, Pam, Sherry and Rodney, words cannot express my sincere thanks for all of your input.

To my Pastor, Vernon Hubbard (Connecting Fellowship), my church family and friends, thank you for your prayers and support, in helping my first book to become a Amazon #1 Bestseller.

To Jennie, thank you for always taking care of my Baby, especially while I was writing this book. Your work is greatly appreciated.

To Kim Porter, my editor, you have been editing for me for more than 25 years now. It is only appropriate that you would edit my book. Thanks for just being Awesome.

ABOUT THE AUTHOR

Business expert and mother of two lovely girls, Debbie Porter, was born into an entrepreneurial family and currently lives in Houston, Texas. The eldest of five children, Debbie wasted no time focusing on her career and professional pursuits to set that perfect pace for her siblings to follow suit. Living in a family where business was always discussed, she began to develop an interest in business, at a young age. Debbie went on to earn a degree in Business Management and has since been involved in numerous for profit and non-profit businesses. With her natural love for and her diverse business expertise, she has helped many companies identify their problems and offer them successful solutions.

Her level of expertise makes her book a must read for aspiring entrepreneurs, startup and early-stage ventures, as well as business owners seeking to expand their current business. Passionate about helping business owners have a successful company with little or no stress at all, Debbie takes intense pleasure in seeing businesses come out of trouble, doing what is needed and succeeding beyond expectations. When she is not Helping other business owners or writing, she enjoys traveling with her husband of 28 years. She loves laughing, living a balanced life, spending time with her family and friends, being involved in various church ministries, as well as playing board games, and watching movies.

Website: www.bookdebbieporter.com

Email: thebusinessrenovator@yahoo.com

www.ingramcontent.com/pod-product-compliance
Lightning Source LLC
Chambersburg PA
CBHW071225170526
45165CB00003B/1000